TWELFTH NIGHT

TWELFTH NIGHT

William Shakespeare

WORDSWORTH CLASSICS

This edition published 1992 by
Wordsworth Editions Limited
8B East Street, Ware, Hertfordshire SG12 9HJ

ISBN 1 85326 010 X

Reprinted 1992

Printed and bound by Clays Limited, Bungay, Suffolk

INTRODUCTION

TWELFTH NIGHT is a classic Shakespearean comedy of mistaken identity, mayhem and the triumph of true love. The identical twins, Viola and Sebastian are parted in a shipwreck, and each believes that the other is drowned. Viola assumes masculine dress, and is employed as a page by Orsino, Duke of Illyria, and acts as a messenger to the Duke's beloved, Olivia, who is in mourning for her dead brother. Olivia rejects Orsino, but thinking Viola to be a young man falls in love with him, though by this stage Viola has fallen in love with Orsino. In time, Sebastian reappears, and Olivia, taking him to be the object of her love, sends for a priest and to his astonishment marries him. Further confusions are cleared up when the Duke yields Olivia to Sebastian, and learning of Viola's love for him turns his affection to her and marries her.

The bitter-sweet, lyrical and melancholy atmosphere of much of the play is offset by the comic sub-plot. This encompasses contrasting members of Olivia's household; Sir Toby Belch, her dissolute uncle, his friend Sir Andrew Aguecheek, the humourless and pompous steward Malvolio who fancies himself worthy of Olivia's hand, the conniving maid Maria and the clown Feste.

The title of the play remains something of a mystery. 'Saw *Twelfth Night* acted well, though it be but a silly play and not related to the name or day' wrote Samuel Pepys. However, it is likely that it was first performed on Twelfth Night, the eve of Epiphany, in 1601 at Whitehall; it was given in the presence of Queen Elizabeth and her guest of honour, an Italian nobleman named Virginio Orsino, after whom the character of the Duke of Illyria was named. Certainly, the cross-dressing and role-reversal in the play is a familiar tradition of winter festivities in many cultures, and is still alive in the modern British pantomime. The alternative title *What You Will* suggests either that the play is only a frothy confection, or that it is simply make-believe in which many wishes are fulfilled.

Twelfth Night is the perfection of romantic comedy, beautifully composed, with the most subtle intermingling of plot, weaving an assured path between the excesses of grand passion and low comedy. Orsino is a real Renaissance lover, a mixture of romantic impulse and ducal prudence, while the over-anxious Malvolio is a tragi-comic figure of almost heroic proportions. His obsessive conscientiousness blinds him to the realities of life, leading him to the astounding belief that he is a plausible candidate for Olivia's hand. The ensuing insults heaped on him by other members of the household culminate in a moving speech of baffled dignity.

Details of William Shakespeare's early life are scanty. He was the son of a prosperous merchant of Stratford upon Avon, and tradition has it that he was born on 23rd April 1564; records show that he was baptized three days later. It is likely that he attended the local Grammar School, but he had no university education. Of his early career there is no record, though John Aubrey states that he was a country schoolmaster. How he became involved with the stage is equally uncertain, but he was sufficiently established as a playwright by 1592 to be criticised in print. He was a leading member of the Lord Chamberlain's Company, which became the King's Men on the accession of James 1 in 1603. Shakespeare married Anne Hathaway in 1582, by whom he had two daughters and a son, Hamnet, who died in 1586. Towards the end of his life he loosened his ties with London, and retired to New Place, his substantial property in Stratford which he had bought in 1597. He died on 23rd April 1616 aged 52, and is buried in Holy Trinity Church, Stratford.

FURTHER READING
L Hotson: The First Night of Twelfth Night 1970
W King: 20th Century Interpretations of Twelfth Night 1968
C Leech: Twelfth Night and Shakespearean Comedy 1965
C T Onions: A Shakespeare Glossary 1962

TWELFTH NIGHT

The scene: Illyria

CHARACTERS IN THE PLAY

ORSINO, *Duke of Illyria*

SEBASTIAN, *brother to Viola*

ANTONIO, *a sea-captain, friend to Sebastian*

Another sea-captain, friend to Viola

VALENTINE ⎫
CURIO ⎭ *gentlemen attending on the Duke*

SIR TOBY BELCH, *kinsman to Olivia*

SIR ANDREW AGUECHEEK

MALVOLIO, *steward to Olivia*

FABIAN, *a gentleman in the service of Olivia*

FESTE, *fool to Olivia*

OLIVIA, *a rich countess*

VIOLA, *in love with the Duke*

MARIA, *Olivia's gentlewoman (small of stature)*

Lords, priests, sailors, officers, musicians, and other attendants

TWELFTH NIGHT:

OR,

WHAT YOU WILL

[I. I.]   *A room in the Duke's palace*

The Duke ORSINO, CURIO *and Lords,*
hearing music; the music ceases

Duke. If music be the food of love, play on,
Give me excess of it; that, surfeiting,
The appetite may sicken, and so die....
That strain again! it had a dying fall:
O, it came o'er my ear like the sweet sound
That breathes upon a bank of violets;
Stealing and giving odour....[*music again*] Enough,
        no more!
'Tis not so sweet now as it was before.
O spirit of love, how quick and fresh art thou,
That, notwithstanding thy capacity   10
Receiveth as the sea, nought enters there,
Of what validity and pitch soe'er,
But falls into abatement and low price,
Even in a minute...So full of shapes is fancy,
That it alone is high fantastical.
Curio. Will you go hunt, my lord?
Duke.   What, Curio?
Curio.   The hart.
Duke. Why, so I do, the noblest that I have:
O, when mine eyes did see Olivia first,
Methought she purged the air of pestilence;
That instant was I turned into a hart,   20
And my desires, like fell and cruel hounds,
E'er since pursue me....

VALENTINE enters

　　　　　　　　How now? what news from her?
Valentine. So please my lord, I might not be admitted,
But from her handmaid do return this answer:
†The element itself, till seven years hence,
Shall not behold her face at ample view;
But like a cloistress she will veiléd walk,
And water once a day her chamber round
With eye-offending brine: all this to season
30 A brother's dead love, which she would keep fresh
And lasting, in her sad remembrance.
　　Duke. O, she that hath a heart of that fine frame
To pay this debt of love but to a brother,
How will she love, when the rich golden shaft
Hath killed the flock of all affections else
That live in her; when liver, brain and heart,
These sovereign thrones, are all supplied and filled,
Her sweet perfections, with one self king!
Away before me to sweet beds of flowers—
40 Love-thoughts lie rich when canopied with bowers.
　　　　　　　　　　　　　　[they go

[I. 2.]　　　　*Near the sea-coast*

VIOLA, Captain, and sailors

　Viola. What country, friends, is this?
　Captain. This is Illyria, lady.
　Viola. And what should I do in Illyria?
My brother he is in Elysium.
Perchance he is not drowned: what think you, sailors?
　Captain. It is perchance that you yourself were saved.
　Viola. O my poor brother! and so perchance may he be.
　Captain. True, madam, and to comfort you
　　　　with chance,
Assure yourself, after our ship did split,

When you and those poor number saved with you   10
Hung on our driving boat...I saw your brother,
Most provident in peril, bind himself—
Courage and hope both teaching him the practice—
To a strong mast that lived upon the sea;
Where, like Arion on the dolphin's back,
I saw him hold acquaintance with the waves
So long as I could see.

Viola.   For saying so, there's gold:
Mine own escape unfoldeth to my hope,
Whereto thy speech serves for authority,
The like of him. Know'st thou this country?   20

Captain. Ay, madam, well, for I was bred and born
Not three hours' travel from this very place.

Viola. Who governs here?

Captain. A noble duke, in nature as in name.

Viola. What is his name?

Captain. Orsino.

Viola. Orsino: I have heard my father name him.
He was a bachelor then.

Captain. And so is now, or was so very late:
For but a month ago I went from hence,   30
And then 'twas fresh in murmur—as, you know,
What great ones do the less will prattle of—
That he did seek the love of fair Olivia.

Viola. What's she?

Captain. A virtuous maid, the daughter of a count
That died some twelvemonth since—then leaving her
In the protection of his son, her brother,
Who shortly also died: for whose dear love,
They say, she hath abjured the company
And sight of men.

Viola.   O, that I served that lady,   40
And might not be delivered to the world,

Till I had made mine own occasion mellow,
What my estate is.

   Captain.   That were hard to compass,
Because she will admit no kind of suit,
No, not the duke's.

   Viola. There is a fair behaviour in thee, captain,
And though that nature with a beauteous wall
Doth oft close in pollution, yet of thee
I will believe thou hast a mind that suits
50 With this thy fair and outward character.
I prithee, and I'll pay thee bounteously,
Conceal me what I am, and be my aid
For such disguise as haply shall become
The form of my intent. I'll serve this duke,
Thou shalt present me as an eunuch to him,
It may be worth thy pains: for I can sing,
And speak to him in many sorts of music,
That will allow me very worth his service.
What else may hap to time I will commit,
60 Only shape thou thy silence to my wit.

   Captain. Be you his eunuch, and your mute I'll be,
When my tongue blabs, then let mine eyes not see!

   Viola. I thank thee: lead me on.   [*they go*

[1. 3.]   *A room in Olivia's house*

*Sir TOBY BELCH seated with drink before him,
and MARIA*

Sir Toby. What a plague means my niece, to take
the death of her brother thus? I am sure care's an
enemy to life.

Maria. By my troth, Sir Toby, you must come in
earlier o' nights: your cousin, my lady, takes great
exceptions to your ill hours.

Sir Toby. Why, let her except before excepted.

Maria. Ay, but you must confine yourself within the modest limits of order.

Sir Toby. Confine? I'll confine myself no finer than 10 I am: these clothes are good enough to drink in, and so be these boots too: an they be not, let them hang themselves in their own straps.

Maria. That quaffing and drinking will undo you: I heard my lady talk of it yesterday: and of a foolish knight, that you brought in one night here, to be her wooer.

Sir Toby. Who? Sir Andrew Aguecheek?

Maria. Ay, he.

Sir Toby. He's as tall a man as any's in Illyria.   20

Maria. What's that to th' purpose?

Sir Toby. Why, he has three thousand ducats a year.

Maria. Ay, but he'll have but a year in all these ducats; he's a very fool and a prodigal.

Sir Toby. Fie, that you'll say so! he plays o'th' viol-de-gamboys, and speaks three or four languages word for word without book, and hath all the good gifts of nature.

Maria. He hath, indeed almost natural: for, besides that he's a fool, he's a great quarreller: and but that he 30 hath the gift of a coward to allay the gust he hath in quarrelling, 'tis thought among the prudent he would quickly have the gift of a grave.

Sir Toby. By this hand, they are scoundrels and sub-stractors that say so of him. Who are they?

Maria. They that add, moreover, he's drunk nightly in your company.

Sir Toby. With drinking healths to my niece: I'll drink to her as long as there is a passage in my throat and drink in Illyria: he's a coward and a coystrill that will not 40

drink to my niece, till his brains turn o'th' toe like a
parish-top....[*he seizes her about the waist and they
dance a turn*] What, wench! †Castiliano vulgo; for here
comes Sir Andrew Agueface.

Sir ANDREW AGUECHEEK enters

Sir Andrew. Sir Toby Belch! how now, Sir Toby
Belch?

Sir Toby. Sweet Sir Andrew!

Sir Andrew. Bless you, fair shrew.

Maria [*curtsies*]. And you too, sir!

50 *Sir Toby.* Accost, Sir Andrew, accost.

Sir Andrew. What's that?

Sir Toby. My niece's chambermaid.

Sir Andrew. Good Mistress Accost, I desire better
acquaintance.

Maria. My name is Mary, sir.

Sir Andrew. Good Mistress Mary Accost,—

(*Sir Toby.* You mistake, knight: 'accost' is front her,
board her, woo her, assail her.

(*Sir Andrew.* By my troth, I would not undertake her
60 in this company. Is that the meaning of 'accost'?

Maria. Fare you well, gentlemen.   [*she turns to go*

(*Sir Toby.* An thou let part so, Sir Andrew, would
thou mightst never draw sword again.

Sir Andrew. An you part so, mistress, I would I might
never draw sword again...Fair lady, do you think you
have fools in hand?

Maria. Sir, I have not you by th'hand

Sir Andrew. Marry, but you shall have—and here's
my hand.   [*he holds it out*

70 *Maria* [*takes it*]. Now, sir, 'thought is free'...[*she
looks at his palm*] I pray you, bring your hand to th'
buttery-bar, and let it drink.

Sir Andrew. Wherefore, sweet-heart? what's your metaphor?

Maria. It's dry, sir.

Sir Andrew. Why, I think so; I am not such an ass, but I can keep my hand dry. But what's your jest?

Maria. A dry jest, sir.

Sir Andrew. Are you full of them?

Maria. Ay, sir; I have them at my fingers' ends: 80 marry, now I let go your hand, I am barren.

[*she drops his hand, curtsies and trips away*

Sir Toby [*sits*]. O knight, thou lack'st a cup of canary: when did I see thee so put down?

Sir Andrew. Never in your life, I think, unless you see canary put me down...[*sits beside him*] Methinks sometimes I have no more wit than a Christian or an ordinary man has: but I am a great eater of beef and I believe that does harm to my wit.

Sir Toby. No question.

Sir Andrew. An I thought that, I'd forswear it. I'll 90 ride home to-morrow, Sir Toby.

Sir Toby. Pourquoi, my dear knight?

Sir Andrew. What is 'pourquoi'? do or not do? I would I had bestowed that time in the tongues, that I have in fencing, dancing and bear-baiting: O, had I but followed the arts!

Sir Toby [*fondles him*]. Then hadst thou had an excellent head of hair.

Sir Andrew. Why, would that have mended my hair?   100

Sir Toby. Past question, for thou seest it will not curl by nature.

Sir Andrew. But it becomes me well enough, does't not?

Sir Toby. Excellent! it hangs like flax on a distaff; and

I hope to see a housewife take thee between her legs and spin it off.

Sir Andrew. Faith, I'll home to-morrow, Sir Toby. Your niece will not be seen, or if she be it's four to one she'll none of me: the count himself here hard by woos her.

Sir Toby. She'll none o'th' count—she'll not match above her degree, neither in estate, years, nor wit; I have heard her swear't. Tut, there's life in't, man.

Sir Andrew. I'll stay a month longer....I am a fellow o'th' strangest mind i'th' world: I delight in masques and revels sometimes altogether.

Sir Toby. Art thou good at these kickshawses, knight?

Sir Andrew. As any man in Illyria, whatsoever he be, under the degree of my betters, and yet I will not compare with an old man.

Sir Toby. What is thy excellence in a galliard, knight?

Sir Andrew. Faith, I can cut a caper.

(Sir Toby. And I can cut the mutton to't.

Sir Andrew. And I think I have the back-trick simply as strong as any man in Illyria.

Sir Toby. Wherefore are these things hid? wherefore have these gifts a curtain before 'em? are they like to take dust, like Mistress Mall's picture? why dost thou not go to church in a galliard and come home in a coranto? My very walk should be a jig; I would not so much as make water but in a sink-a-pace. What dost thou mean? Is it a world to hide virtues in? I did think, by the excellent constitution of thy leg, it was formed under the star of a galliard.

Sir Andrew. Ay, 'tis strong, and it does indifferent well in a †dun-coloured stock. Shall we set about some revels?

Sir Toby. What shall we do else? were we not born under Taurus?

Sir Andrew. Taurus! That's sides and heart.   140

Sir Toby. No, sir, it is legs and thighs...Let me see thee caper [*Sir Andrew leaps*]....Ha! higher: ha, ha! excellent!   [*they go*

[1. 4.]   *A room in the Duke's palace*

'*Enter VALENTINE, and VIOLA in man's attire*'

Valentine. If the duke continue these favours towards you, Cesario, you are like to be much advanced. He hath known you but three days, and already you are no stranger.

Viola. You either fear his humour or my negligence, that you call in question the continuance of his love. Is he inconstant, sir, in his favours?

Valentine. No, believe me.

Viola. I thank you. Here comes the count.

'*Enter DUKE, CURIO and attendants*'

Duke. Who saw Cesario, ho!   10

Viola. On your attendance, my lord, here.

Duke. Stand you awhile aloof....[*Curio and attendants withdraw*] Cesario,

Thou know'st no less but all: I have unclasped
To thee the book even of my secret soul.
Therefore, good youth, address thy gait unto her,
Be not denied access, stand at her doors,
And tell them, there thy fixéd foot shall grow
Till thou have audience.

Viola.   Sure, my noble lord,
If she be so abandoned to her sorrow
As it is spoke, she never will admit me.   20

Duke. Be clamorous and leap all civil bounds
Rather than make unprofited return.

Viola. Say I do speak with her, my lord, what then?
Duke. O, then unfold the passion of my love,
Surprise her with discourse of my dear faith:
It shall become thee well to act my woes;
She will attend it better in thy youth
Than in a nuncio's of more grave aspect.
Viola. I think not so, my lord.
Duke.   Dear lad, believe it;
30 For they shall yet belie thy happy years,
That say thou art a man: Diana's lip
Is not more smooth and rubious; thy small pipe
Is as the maiden's organ, shrill and sound—
And all is semblative a woman's part.
I know thy constellation is right apt
For this affair...[*he beckons attendants*] Some four or
          five attend him,
All if you will; for I myself am best
When least in company...Prosper well in this,
And thou shalt live as freely as thy lord,
40 To call his fortunes thine.
Viola.   I'll do my best,
To woo your lady...[*aside*] Yet, a barful strife!
Whoe'er I woo, myself would be his wife.   [*they go*

[1. 5.]   *A room in Olivia's house; at the
                    back a chair of state*

MARIA and CLOWN

Maria. Nay, either tell me where thou hast been, or
I will not open my lips so wide as a bristle may enter
in way of thy excuse: my lady will hang thee for thy
absence.

Clown. Let her hang me: he that is well hanged in this
world needs to fear no colours.

Maria. Make that good.

Clown. He shall see none to fear.

Maria. A good lenten answer: I can tell thee where that saying was born, of 'I fear no colours.'   10

Clown. Where, good Mistress Mary?

Maria. In the wars—and that may you be bold to say in your foolery.

Clown. Well, God give them wisdom that have it; and those that are fools, let them use their talents.

Maria. Yet you will be hanged for being so long absent; or to be turned away, is not that as good as a hanging to you?

Clown. Many a good hanging prevents a bad marriage; and, for turning away, let summer bear it out.   20

Maria. You are resolute, then?

Clown. Not so neither, but I am resolved on two points—

Maria. That if one break, the other will hold; or if both break, your gaskins fall.

Clown. Apt in good faith, very apt...[*she turns to go*] Well, go thy way—if Sir Toby would leave drinking, thou wert as witty a piece of Eve's flesh as any in Illyria.

Maria. Peace, you rogue, no more o' that: here comes my lady: make your excuse wisely, you were best.   30

[*she goes*

The Lady OLIVIA *enters in black,* MALVOLIO *and attendants following; she sits in her chair of state*

Clown [*feigns not to see them*]. Wit, an't be thy will, put me into good fooling! Those wits that think they have thee, do very oft prove fools; and I, that am sure I lack thee, may pass for a wise man. For what says Quinapalus? 'Better a witty fool than a foolish wit.' [*turns*] God bless thee, lady!

Olivia. Take the fool away.

Clown. Do you not hear, fellows? Take away the lady.

Olivia. Go to, y'are a dry fool: I'll no more of you:
40 besides, you grow dishonest.

Clown. Two faults, madonna, that drink and good
counsel will amend: for give the dry fool drink, then is
the fool not dry: bid the dishonest man mend himself; if
he mend, he is no longer dishonest; if he cannot, let the
botcher mend him: any thing that's mended is but
patched: virtue that transgresses, is but patched with sin,
and sin that amends is but patched with virtue....If that
this simple syllogism will serve, so: if it will not, what
remedy? As there is no true cuckold but calamity, so
50 beauty's a flower: the lady bade take away the fool,
therefore I say again, take her away.

Olivia. Sir, I bade them take away you.

Clown. Misprision in the highest degree! Lady,
'Cucullus non facit monachum'; that's as much to say
as I wear not motley in my brain...Good madonna, give
me leave to prove you a fool.

Olivia. Can you do it?

Clown. Dexteriously, good madonna.

Olivia. Make your proof.

60 *Clown.* I must catechize you for it, madonna. Good
my mouse of virtue, answer me.

Olivia. Well, sir, for want of other idleness, I'll bide
your proof.

Clown. Good madonna, why mourn'st thou?

Olivia. Good fool, for my brother's death.

Clown. I think his soul is in hell, madonna.

Olivia. I know his soul is in heaven, fool.

Clown. The more fool, madonna, to mourn for
your brother's soul, being in heaven....Take away the
70 fool, gentlemen.

Olivia. What think you of this fool, Malvolio? doth he not mend?

Malvolio. Yes, and shall do, till the pangs of death shake him: infirmity, that decays the wise, doth ever make the better fool.

Clown. God send you, sir, a speedy infirmity, for the better increasing your folly! Sir Toby will be sworn that I am no fox, but he will not pass his word for two pence that you are no fool.

Olivia. How say you to that, Malvolio? 80

Malvolio. I marvel your ladyship takes delight in such a barren rascal: I saw him put down the other day with an ordinary fool that has no more brain than a stone. Look you now, he's out of his guard already; unless you laugh and minister occasion to him, he is gagged. I protest, I take these wise men, that crow so at these set kind of fools, no better than the fools' zanies.

Olivia. O, you are sick of self-love, Malvolio, and taste with a distempered appetite. To be generous, guiltless, and of free disposition, is to take those things 90 for bird-bolts that you deem cannon-bullets: there is no slander in an allowed fool, though he do nothing but rail; nor no railing in a known discreet man, though he do nothing but reprove.

Clown. Now Mercury endue thee with leasing, for thou speakest well of fools!

MARIA returns

Maria. Madam, there is at the gate a young gentleman much desires to speak with you.

Olivia. From the Count Orsino, is it?

Maria. I know not, madam—'tis a fair young man, and 100 well attended.

Olivia. Who of my people hold him in delay?

Maria. Sir Toby, madam, your kinsman.

Olivia. Fetch him off, I pray you! he speaks nothing but madman: fie on him....[*Maria hurries away*] Go you, Malvolio: if it be a suit from the count, I am sick, or not at home....what you will, to dismiss it. [*Malvolio goes*] Now you see, sir, how your fooling grows old, and people dislike it.

110 *Clown.* Thou hast spoke for us, madonna, as if thy eldest son should be a fool: whose skull Jove cram with brains! for—here he comes—one of thy kin, has a most weak pia mater.

Sir TOBY BELCH staggers in

Olivia. By mine honour, half drunk....What is he at the gate, cousin?

Sir Toby [*speaks thick*]. A gentleman.

Olivia. A gentleman? What gentleman?

Sir Toby. 'Tis a gentleman here...[*hiccoughs*] A plague o'these pickle-herring....[*Clown laughs*] How 120 now, sot!

Clown. Good Sir Toby—

Olivia. Cousin, cousin, how have you come so early by this lethargy?

Sir Toby. Lechery! I defy lechery...There's one at the gate.

Olivia. Ay, marry, what is he?

Sir Toby. Let him be the devil, an he will, I care not: give me 'faith,' say I....[*he totters to the door*] Well, it's all one.   [*he goes*

130 *Olivia.* What's a drunken man like, fool?

Clown. Like a drowned man, a fool, and a mad man: one draught above heat makes him a fool, the second mads him, and a third drowns him.

Olivia. Go thou and seek the crowner, and let him

sit o' my coz; for he's in the third degree of drink: he's drowned: go look after him.

Clown. He is but mad yet, madonna, and the fool shall look to the madman.   [*he follows Sir Toby*

MALVOLIO *returns*

Malvolio. Madam, yon young fellow swears he will speak with you. I told him you were sick, he takes on 140 him to understand so much, and therefore comes to speak with you. I told him you were asleep, he seems to have a foreknowledge of that too, and therefore comes to speak with you. What is to be said to him, lady? he's fortified against any denial.

Olivia. Tell him he shall not speak with me.

Malvolio. Has been told so; and he says he'll stand at your door like a sheriff's post, and be the supporter to a bench, but he'll speak with you.

Olivia. What kind o' man is he?   150

Malvolio. Why, of mankind.

Olivia. What manner of man?

Malvolio. Of very ill manner; he'll speak with you, will you, or no.

Olivia. Of what personage and years is he?

Malvolio. Not yet old enough for a man, nor young enough for a boy; as a squash is before 'tis a peascod, or a codling when 'tis almost an apple: 'tis with him in standing water between boy and man. He is very well-favoured and he speaks very shrewishly; one would 160 think his mother's milk were scarce out of him.

Olivia. Let him approach...Call in my gentlewoman.

Malvolio [*goes to the door*]. Gentlewoman, my lady calls.   [*he departs*

MARIA returns

Olivia. Give me my veil: come, throw it o'er my face—
We'll once more hear Orsino's embassy. [*Maria veils her*

VIOLA (as Cesario) enters

Viola. The honourable lady of the house, which is
she?

170 *Olivia.* Speak to me, I shall answer for her: your will?

Viola. Most radiant, exquisite, and unmatchable
beauty!—I pray you, tell me if this be the lady of the
house, for I never saw her. I would be loath to cast
away my speech; for besides that it is excellently well
penned, I have taken great pains to con it. Good
beauties, let me sustain no scorn; I am very comptible,
even to the least sinister usage.

Olivia. Whence came you, sir?

Viola. I can say little more than I have studied, and
180 that question's out of my part. Good gentle one, give
me modest assurance if you be the lady of the house,
that I may proceed in my speech.

Olivia. Are you a comedian?

Viola. No, my profound heart: and yet, by the very
fangs of malice I swear, I am not that I play. Are you
the lady of the house?

Olivia. If I do not usurp myself, I am.

Viola. Most certain, if you are she, you do usurp yourself; for what is yours to bestow, is not yours to reserve.
190 But this is from my commission: I will on with my
speech in your praise, and then show you the heart of my
message.

Olivia. Come to what is important in't: I forgive you
the praise.

Viola. Alas, I took great pains to study it, and 'tis
poetical.

Olivia. It is the more like to be feigned, I pray you keep it in. I heard you were saucy at my gates, and allowed your approach rather to wonder at you than to hear you. If you be not mad, be gone; if you have 200 reason, be brief: 'tis not that time of moon with me to make one in so skipping a dialogue.

Maria [*points to the hat in Viola's hand*]. Will you hoist sail, sir? here lies your way.

[*she opens the door to thrust her out*

Viola [*resists*]. No, good swabber; I am to hull here a little longer....Some mollification for your giant, sweet lady!

Olivia. Tell me your mind.

Viola. I am a messenger.

Olivia. Sure, you have some hideous matter to deliver, 210 when the courtesy of it is so fearful. Speak your office.

Viola. It alone concerns your ear. I bring no overture of war, no taxation of homage; I hold the olive in my hand: my words are as full of peace as matter.

Olivia. Yet you began rudely. What are you? what would you?

Viola. The rudeness that hath appeared in me have I learned from my entertainment. What I am, and what I would, are as secret as maidenhead: to your ears, 220 divinity; to any other's, profanation.

Olivia. Give us the place alone: we will hear this divinity....[*Maria and attendants withdraw*] Now, sir, what is your text?

Viola. Most sweet lady,—

Olivia. A comfortable doctrine, and much may be said of it. Where lies your text?

Viola. In Orsino's bosom.

Olivia. In his bosom! In what chapter of his bosom?

230 *Viola.* To answer by the method, in the first of his heart.

Olivia. O, I have read it; it is heresy. Have you no more to say?

Viola. Good madam, let me see your face.

Olivia. Have you any commission from your lord to negotiate with my face? you are now out of your text: but we will draw the curtain, and show you the picture....
[*she unveils*] Look you, sir, such a one I was—this present! Is't not well done?

240 *Viola.* Excellently done, if God did all.

Olivia. 'Tis in grain, sir, 'twill endure wind and weather.

Viola. 'Tis beauty truly blent, whose red and white
Nature's own sweet and cunning hand laid on:
Lady, you are the cruell'st she alive,
If you will lead these graces to the grave,
And leave the world no copy.

Olivia. O, sir, I will not be so hard-hearted; I will give out divers schedules of my beauty: it shall be in-
250 ventoried, and every particle and utensil labelled to my will: as, *Item,* Two lips indifferent red; *Item,* Two grey eyes with lids to them; *Item,* One neck, one chin, and so forth. Were you sent hither to praise me?

Viola. I see you what you are, you are too proud;
But, if you were the devil, you are fair...
My lord and master loves you; O, such love
Could be but recompensed, though you were crowned
The nonpareil of beauty!

Olivia. How does he love me?

Viola. With adorations, fertile tears,
260 With groans that thunder love, with sighs of fire.

Olivia. Your lord does know my mind, I cannot love him:

Yet I suppose him virtuous, know him noble,
Of great estate, of fresh and stainless youth;
In voices well divulged, free, learned and valiant,
And in dimension and the shape of nature
A gracious person: but yet I cannot love him;
He might have took his answer long ago.

Viola. If I did love you in my master's flame,
With such a suff'ring, such a deadly life,
In your denial I would find no sense,   270
I would not understand it.

Olivia.   Why, what would you?

Viola. Make me a willow cabin at your gate,
And call upon my soul within the house,
Write loyal cantons of contemnéd love,
And sing them loud even in the dead of night;
Holla your name to the reverberate hills,
And make the babbling gossip of the air
Cry out 'Olivia!' O, you should not rest
Between the elements of air and earth,
But you should pity me.

Olivia.   You might do much: 280
What is your parentage?

Viola. Above my fortunes, yet my state is well:
I am a gentleman.

Olivia.   Get you to your lord;
I cannot love him: let him send no more,
Unless—perchance—you come to me again,
To tell me how he takes it...Fare you well:
I thank you for your pains: spend this for me.

                              [*offers money*

Viola. I am no fee'd post, lady; keep your purse.
My master, not myself, lacks recompense.
Love make his heart of flint that you shall love,   290
And let your fervour like my master's be

Placed in contempt! Farewell, fair cruelty.   [*she goes*
  Olivia. 'What is your parentage?'
'Above my fortunes, yet my state is well:
I am a gentleman'....I'll be sworn thou art!
Thy tongue, thy face, thy limbs, actions, and spirit,
Do give thee five-fold blazon...Not too fast: soft! soft!
Unless the master were the man....[*she muses*] How now!
Even so quickly may one catch the plague?
300 Methinks I feel this youth's perfections
With an invisible and subtle stealth
To creep in at mine eyes....Well, let it be....
What, ho, Malvolio!

MALVOLIO *returns*

  Malvolio.   Here, madam, at your service.
  Olivia. Run after that same peevish messenger,
The county's man: he left this ring behind him,
Would I or not; tell him I'll none of it.
Desire him not to flatter with his lord,
Nor hold him up with hopes—I am not for him:
If that the youth will come this way to-morrow,
310 I'll give him reasons for't...Hie thee, Malvolio.
  Malvolio. Madam, I will.   [*he hurries forth*
  Olivia. I do I know not what, and fear to find
Mine eye too great a flatterer for my mind...
Fate, show thy force—ourselves we do not owe—
What is decreed, must be; and be this so!   [*she goes*

[2. 1.]   *At the door of Antonio's house*

ANTONIO *and* SEBASTIAN

Antonio. Will you stay no longer? nor will you not
that I go with you?
  Sebastian. By your patience, no: my stars shine darkly

over me; the malignancy of my fate might perhaps distemper yours; therefore I shall crave of you your leave that I may bear my evils alone: it were a bad recompense for your love, to lay any of them on you.

Antonio. Let me yet know of you whither you are bound.

Sebastian. No, sooth, sir: my determinate voyage is 10 mere extravagancy. But I perceive in you so excellent a touch of modesty, that you will not extort from me what I am willing to keep in; therefore it charges me in manners the rather to express myself...You must know of me then, Antonio, my name is Sebastian, which I called Roderigo. My father was that Sebastian of Messaline, whom I know you have heard of. He left behind him myself and a sister, both born in an hour: if the heavens had been pleased, would we had so ended! But you, sir, altered that, for some hour before you took 20 me from the breach of the sea was my sister drowned.

Antonio. Alas, the day!

Sebastian. A lady, sir, though it was said she much resembled me, was yet of many accounted beautiful: but, though I could not with such estimable wonder overfar believe that, yet thus far I will boldly publish her—she bore a mind that envy could not but call fair...She is drowned already, sir, with salt water, though I seem to drown her remembrance again with more.

Antonio. Pardon me, sir, your bad entertainment. 30

Sebastian. O, good Antonio, forgive me your trouble.

Antonio. If you will not murder me for my love, let me be your servant.

Sebastian. If you will not undo what you have done, that is, kill him whom you have recovered, desire it not. Fare ye well at once. My bosom is full of kindness, and I am yet so near the manners of my mother, that upon

the least occasion more mine eyes will tell tales of me...
[*they clasp hands*] I am bound to the Count Orsino's
40 court—farewell!   [*he goes*

Antonio. The gentleness of all the gods go with thee!
I have many enemies in Orsino's court,
Else would I very shortly see thee there:
But, come what may, I do adore thee so,
That danger shall seem sport, and I will go. [*he goes in*

[2. 2.]   *A street near Olivia's house*

    VIOLA approaches, MALVOLIO following after

Malvolio [*comes up*]. Were not you e'en now with the
Countess Olivia?

Viola. Even now, sir. On a moderate pace I have
since arrived but hither.

Malvolio [*sharply*]. She returns this ring to you, sir;
you might have saved me my pains, to have taken it
away yourself. She adds moreover, that you should put
your lord into a desperate assurance she will none of
him: and one thing more, that you be never so hardy to
10 come again in his affairs, unless it be to report your lord's
taking of this...[*he holds out the ring*] Receive it so.

Viola. She took the ring of me...I'll none of it.

Malvolio. Come, sir, you peevishly threw it to her;
and her will is, it should be so returned: [*he throws it
at her feet*] if it be worth stooping for, there it lies in
your eye; if not, be it his that finds it.   [*he walks off*

Viola. I left no ring with her: what means this lady?
Fortune forbid my outside have not charmed her!
She made good view of me, indeed so much,
20 That as methought her eyes had lost her tongue,
For she did speak in starts distractedly....
She loves me, sure—the cunning of her passion

Invites me in this churlish messenger...
None of my lord's ring! why, he sent her none...
I am the man—if it be so, as 'tis,
Poor lady, she were better love a dream...
Disguise, I see thou art a wickedness,
Wherein the pregnant enemy does much.
How easy is it for the proper-false
In women's waxen hearts to set their forms!   30
Alas, our frailty is the cause, not we,
For such as we are made of, such we be...
How will this fadge? My master loves her dearly,
And I (poor monster!) fond as much on him:
And she, mistaken, seems to dote on me:
What will become of this? As I am man,
My state is desperate for my master's love;
As I am woman—now alas the day!—
What thriftless sighs shall poor Olivia breathe?
O time, thou must untangle this, not I,   40
It is too hard a knot for me t'untie.   [*she goes*

[2. 3.] *A room in Olivia's house; a bench and a table*
      with cold viands and drinking-vessels thereon

    Sir TOBY BELCH and Sir ANDREW AGUECHEEK
               enter, drunk

Sir Toby [*sits at table*]. Approach, Sir Andrew: [*Sir Andrew follows with difficulty*] not to be a-bed after midnight is to be up betimes; and 'diluculo surgere,' thou know'st,—

Sir Andrew [*sits beside him*]. Nay, by my troth, I know not: but I know, to be up late is to be up late.
                             [*he eats*

Sir Toby [*takes up a pot and finds it empty*]. A false conclusion: I hate it as an unfilled can. To be up after

midnight and to go to bed then, is early; so that to go to
10 bed after midnight is to go to bed betimes. Does not our
life consist of the four elements?

Sir Andrew [*his mouth full*]. Faith, so they say—but
I think it rather consists of eating and drinking.

Sir Toby. Th'art a scholar; let us therefore eat and
drink. [*bawls*] Marian, I say! a stoup of wine!

The CLOWN comes in

Sir Andrew. Here comes the fool, i'faith.

Clown [*sits between them upon the bench*]. How now,
my hearts! Did you never see the picture of 'we
three'?

20 *Sir Toby*. Welcome, ass. Now let's have a catch.

Sir Andrew. By my troth, the fool has an excellent
breast. I had rather than forty shillings I had such a leg,
and so sweet a breath to sing, as the fool has. In sooth,
thou wast in very gracious fooling last night, when thou
spok'st of Pigrogromitus, of the Vapians passing the
equinoctial of Queubus; 'twas very good, i'faith...
I sent thee sixpence for thy leman—hadst it?

Clown. I did impetticoat thy gratillity: for Malvolio's
nose is no whipstock: my lady has a white hand, and the
30 Myrmidons are no bottle-ale houses.

Sir Andrew. Excellent! why, this is the best fooling,
when all is done. Now, a song.

Sir Toby. Come on, there is sixpence for you. Let's
have a song.

Sir Andrew. There's a testril of me too: if one knight
give a—

Clown. Would you have a love-song, or a song of
good life?

Sir Toby. A love-song, a love-song.

40 *Sir Andrew*. Ay, ay. I care not for good life.

Clown [*sings*].

> O mistress mine, where are you roaming?
> O, stay and hear, your true love's coming,
>   That can sing both high and low.
> Trip no further pretty sweeting:
> Journeys end in lovers meeting,
>   Every wise man's son doth know.

Sir Andrew. Excellent good, i'faith!

Sir Toby. Good, good.

Clown [*sings*].

> What is love, 'tis not hereafter,
> Present mirth hath present laughter: 50
>   What's to come is still unsure.
> In delay there lies no plenty,
> Then come kiss me, sweet and twenty:
>   Youth's a stuff will not endure.

Sir Andrew. A mellifluous voice, as I am true knight.

Sir Toby. A contagious breath.

Sir Andrew. Very sweet and contagious, i'faith.

Sir Toby. To hear by the nose, it is dulcet in contagion....But shall we make the welkin dance indeed? 60 Shall we rouse the night-owl in a catch, that will draw three souls out of one weaver? shall we do that?

Sir Andrew. An you love me, let's do't: I am dog at a catch.

Clown. By'r lady, sir, and some dogs will catch well.

Sir Andrew. Most certain...Let our catch be, 'Thou knave.'

Clown. 'Hold thy peace, thou knave,' knight? I shall be constrained in't to call thee knave, knight.

Sir Andrew. 'Tis not the first time I have constrained 70 one to call me knave. Begin, fool; it begins, 'Hold thy peace.'

Clown. I shall never begin if I hold my peace.

Sir Andrew. Good, i'faith! Come, begin.

                               [they sing the catch

MARIA enters with wine

Maria. What a caterwauling do you keep here! If my lady have not called up her steward Malvolio and bid him turn you out of doors, never trust me.

Sir Toby. 'My lady''s a Cataian, we are politicians, Malvolio's a Peg-a-Ramsey, and

80   *[sings]* 'Three merry men be we.'

Am not I consanguineous? am I not of her blood? Tillyvally! 'lady'!

    [sings] 'There dwelt a man in Babylon,

              Lady, lady!'

Clown. Beshrew me, the knight's in admirable fooling.

Sir Andrew. Ay, he does well enough, if he be disposed, and so do I too; he does it with a better grace, but I do it more natural.

Sir Toby [*sings*]. 'O' the twelfth day of December,'—

90 *Maria.* For the love o' God, peace.

MALVOLIO enters

Malvolio. My masters, are you mad? or what are you? Have you no wit, manners, nor honesty, but to gabble like tinkers at this time of night? Do ye make an alehouse of my lady's house, that ye squeak out your coziers' catches without any mitigation or remorse of voice? Is there no respect of place, persons, nor time in you?

Sir Toby. We did keep time, sir, in our catches. Sneck up!

Malvolio. Sir Toby, I must be round with you. My

100 lady bade me tell you, that, though she harbours you as her kinsman, she's nothing allied to your disorders. If

you can separate yourself and your misdemeanours, you
are welcome to the house; if not, an it would please you
to take leave of her, she is very willing to bid you
farewell.

Sir Toby [*sings to Maria*]. 'Farewell, dear heart, since
I must needs be gone.'   [*he embraces her*

Maria. Nay, good Sir Toby.

Clown [*sings*]. 'His eyes do show his days are almost
done.'   110

Malvolio. Is't even so?

Sir Toby [*sings*]. 'But I will never die.'
                                         [*he falls to the ground*

Clown [*sings*]. Sir Toby, there you lie.

Malvolio. This is much credit to you.

Sir Toby [*rising, sings*]. 'Shall I bid him go?'

Clown [*sings*]. 'What an if you do?'

Sir Toby [*sings*]. 'Shall I bid him go, and spare not?'

Clown [*sings*]. 'O no, no, no, no, you dare not.'

Sir Toby [*to Clown*]. Out o' tune, sir! ye lie…[*to
Malvolio*] Art any more than a steward? Dost thou 120
think because thou art virtuous, there shall be no more
cakes and ale?

Clown. Yes, by Saint Anne, and ginger shall be hot
i'th' mouth too.

Sir Toby. Th'art i'th' right….Go, sir, rub your chain
with crumbs….A stoup of wine, Maria!
                                     [*she fills their vessels*

Malvolio. Mistress Mary, if you prized my lady's
favour at any thing more than contempt, you would not
give means for this uncivil rule; she shall know of it, by
this hand.   [*he departs* 130

Maria. Go shake your ears.

Sir Andrew. 'Twere as good a deed as to drink when
a man's a-hungry, to challenge him the field, and

then to break promise with him and make a fool of him.

Sir Toby. Do't, knight. I'll write thee a challenge; or I'll deliver thy indignation to him by word of mouth.

Maria. Sweet Sir Toby, be patient for to-night: since the youth of the count's was to-day with my lady, she is 140 much out of quiet. For Monsieur Malvolio, let me alone with him: if I do not gull him into a nayword, and make him a common recreation, do not think I have wit enough to lie straight in my bed: I know I can do it.

Sir Toby. Possess us, possess us, tell us something of him.

Maria. Marry, sir, sometimes he is a kind of puritan.

Sir Andrew. O, if I thought that, I'd beat him like a dog.

Sir Toby. What, for being a puritan? thy exquisite 150 reason, dear knight?

Sir Andrew. I have no exquisite reason for't, but I have reason good enough.

Maria. The devil a puritan that he is, or any thing constantly but a time-pleaser, an affectioned ass, that cons state without book and utters it by great swarths: the best persuaded of himself, so crammed, as he thinks, with excellencies, that it is his ground of faith that all that look on him love him; and on that vice in him will my revenge find notable cause to work.

160 *Sir Toby.* What wilt thou do?

Maria. I will drop in his way some obscure epistles of love, wherein by the colour of his beard, the shape of his leg, the manner of his gait, the expressure of his eye, forehead, and complexion, he shall find himself most feelingly personated. I can write very like my lady your niece, on a forgotten matter we can hardly make distinction of our hands.

Sir Toby. Excellent! I smell a device.

Sir Andrew. I have't in my nose too.

Sir Toby. He shall think by the letters that thou wilt 170 drop that they come from my niece, and that she's in love with him.

Maria. My purpose is, indeed, a horse of that colour.

Sir Andrew. And your horse now would make him an ass.

Maria. Ass, I doubt not.

Sir Andrew. O, 'twill be admirable.

Maria. Sport royal, I warrant you: I know my physic will work with him. I will plant you two, and let the fool make a third, where he shall find the letter: observe 180 his construction of it...For this night, to bed, and dream on the event...Farewell.   [*she goes out*

Sir Toby. Good night, Penthesilea.

Sir Andrew. Before me, she's a good wench.

Sir Toby. She's a beagle, true-bred, and one that adores me...what o' that?   [*he sighs*

Sir Andrew. I was adored once too.   [*he sighs also*

Sir Toby. Let's to bed, knight....Thou hadst need send for more money.

Sir Andrew. If I cannot recover your niece, I am a 190 foul way out.

Sir Toby. Send for money knight, if thou hast her not i'th'end, call me cut.

Sir Andrew. If I do not, never trust me, take it how you will.

Sir Toby. Come, come, I'll go burn some sack, 'tis too late to go to bed now: come knight; come knight.

               [*they go*

[2. 4.]   *A room in the Duke's palace*

'*Enter* DUKE, VIOLA, CURIO *and others*'

Duke [*to Viola*]. Give me some music...Now—
      [*musicians enter*] good morrow, friends....
Now, good Cesario, but that piece of song,
That old and antic song we heard last night:
Methought it did relieve my passion much,
More than light airs and recollected terms
Of these most brisk and giddy-pacéd times.
Come, but one verse.

      Curio. He is not here, so please your lordship, that
should sing it.

10 *Duke*. Who was it?

      Curio. Feste, the jester, my lord, a fool that the Lady
Olivia's father took much delight in. He is about the
house.

      Duke. Seek him out, and play the tune the while.
                              [*Curio goes; music plays*
Come hither, boy—if ever thou shalt love,
In the sweet pangs of it remember me:
For, such as I am all true lovers are,
Unstaid and skittish in all motions else,
Save in the constant image of the creature
20 That is beloved....How dost thou like this tune?

      Viola. It gives a very echo to the seat
Where Love is throned.

      Duke.   Thou dost speak masterly.
My life upon't, young though thou art, thine eye
Hath stayed upon some favour that it loves:
Hath it not, boy?

      Viola.   A little, by your favour.

      Duke. What kind of woman is't?

      Viola.   Of your complexion.

Duke. She is not worth thee then. What years,
i'faith?

Viola. About your years, my lord.

Duke. Too old, by heaven: let still the woman take
An elder than herself; so wears she to him,   30
So sways she level in her husband's heart:
For, boy, however we do praise ourselves,
Our fancies are more giddy and unfirm,
More longing, wavering, sooner lost and won,
Than women's are.

Viola.   I think it well, my lord.

Duke. Then let thy love be younger than thyself,
Or thy affection cannot hold the bent:
For women are as roses, whose fair flower
Being once displayed doth fall that very hour.

Viola. And so they are: alas, that they are so;   40
To die, even when they to perfection grow!

CURIO re-enters with CLOWN

Duke. O fellow, come, the song we had last night...
Mark it, Cesario, it is old and plain:
The spinsters and the knitters in the sun,
And the free maids that weave their thread with bones
Do use to chant it; it is silly sooth,
And dallies with the innocence of love,
Like the old age.

Clown. Are you ready, sir?

Duke. Ay, prithee, sing.   [*music* 50

Clown [*sings*].

  Come away, come away death,
  And in sad cypress let me be laid:
   Fly away, fly away breath,
  I am slain by a fair cruel maid:

My shroud of white, stuck all with yew,
    O, prepare it!
My part of death no one so true
    Did share it.

Not a flower, not a flower sweet
60 On my black coffin let there be strown:
    Not a friend, not a friend greet
My poor corpse, where my bones shall be thrown:
A thousand thousand sighs to save,
    Lay me O where
Sad true lover never find my grave,
    To weep there.

Duke [*gives money*]. There's for thy pains.
Clown. No pains, sir, I take pleasure in singing, sir.
Duke. I'll pay thy pleasure then.
70 *Clown.* Truly, sir, and pleasure will be paid, one time or another.
Duke. Give me now leave to leave thee.
Clown. Now, the melancholy god protect thee, and the tailor make thy doublet of changeable taffeta, for thy mind is a very opal. I would have men of such constancy put to sea, that their business might be every thing and their intent every where, for that's it that always makes a good voyage of nothing....Farewell. [*he goes*
Duke. Let all the rest give place...

              [*Curio and attendants depart*
              Once more, Cesario,
80 Get thee to yon same sovereign cruelty:
Tell her, my love, more noble than the world,
Prizes not quantity of dirty lands;
The parts that fortune hath bestowed upon her,
Tell her, I hold as giddily as fortune;
But 'tis that miracle and queen of gems
That nature pranks her in attracts my soul.

Viola. But if she cannot love you, sir?

Duke. I cannot be so answered.

Viola.   Sooth, but you must.
Say that some lady, as perhaps there is,
Hath for your love as great a pang of heart   90
As you have for Olivia: you cannot love her;
You tell her so; must she not then be answered?

Duke. There is no woman's sides
Can bide the beating of so strong a passion
As love doth give my heart: no woman's heart
So big, to hold so much, they lack retention.
Alas, their love may be called appetite—
No motion of the liver, but the palate—
That suffers surfeit, cloyment and revolt;
But mine is all as hungry as the sea,   100
And can digest as much. Make no compare
Between that love a woman can bear me
And that I owe Olivia.

Viola.   Ay, but I know—

Duke. What dost thou know?

Viola. Too well what love women to men may owe:
In faith they are as true of heart as we.
My father had a daughter loved a man,
As it might be, perhaps, were I a woman,
I should your lordship.

Duke.   And what's her history?

Viola. A blank, my lord: she never told her love,   110
But let concealment like a worm i'th' bud
Feed on her damask cheek: she pined in thought,
And with a green and yellow melancholy
She sat like Patience on a monument,
Smiling at grief. Was not this love, indeed?
We men may say more, swear more—but indeed
Our shows are more than will; for still we prove

Much in our vows, but little in our love.

Duke. But died thy sister of her love, my boy?

120 *Viola.* I am all the daughters of my father's house,
And all the brothers too...and yet I know not....

[*they muse*

Sir, shall I to this lady?

Duke [*starts and rouses*]. Ay, that's the theme.
To her in haste; give her this jewel; say,
My love can give no place, bide no denay.   [*they go*

[2. 5.] *A walled garden adjoining the house of Olivia;
two doors, one leading out of the garden, the other opening
into the house whence there runs a broad walk with
great box-trees on either side and a stone seat next the
wall*

The house-door opens and Sir TOBY BELCH *comes
out with Sir* ANDREW AGUECHEEK

Sir Toby [*turns and calls*]. Come thy ways, Signior
Fabian.

Fabian [*follows through the door*]. Nay, I'll come: if
I lose a scruple of this sport, let me be boiled to death
with melancholy.

Sir Toby. Wouldst thou not be glad to have the nig-
gardly rascally sheep-biter come by some notable shame?

Fabian. I would exult, man: you know, he brought
me out o' favour with my lady about a bear-baiting here.

10 *Sir Toby.* To anger him, we'll have the bear again,
and we will fool him black and blue—shall we not, Sir
Andrew?

Sir Andrew. An we do not, it is pity of our lives.

MARIA appears, hurrying down the walk

Sir Toby. Here comes the little villain...How now,
my metal of India?

Maria. Get ye all three into the box-tree: Malvolio's coming down this walk, he has been yonder i'the sun practising behaviour to his own shadow this half hour: observe him, for the love of mockery; for I know this letter will make a contemplative idiot of him. Close, in 20 the name of jesting! [*the men hide in a box-tree*] Lie thou there [*throws down a letter*]...for here comes the trout that must be caught with tickling.

[*she goes within*

MALVOLIO, in plumed hat, comes slowly along the path, musing

Malvolio. 'Tis but fortune, all is fortune....Maria once told me she did affect me, and I have heard herself come thus near, that should she fancy it should be one of my complexion....Besides, she uses me with a more exalted respect than any one else that follows her....What should I think on't?

(*Sir Toby.* Here's an overweening rogue!   30

(*Fabian.* O, peace! Contemplation makes a rare turkey-cock of him. How he jets under his advanced plumes!

(*Sir Andrew.* 'Slight, I could so beat the rogue!

(*Fabian.* Peace, I say.

Malvolio. To be Count Malvolio!

(*Sir Toby.* Ah, rogue!

(*Sir Andrew.* Pistol him, pistol him.

(*Fabian.* Peace, peace!

Malvolio. There is example for't; the lady of the Strachy married the yeoman of the wardrobe.   40

(*Sir Andrew.* Fie on him, Jezebel!

(*Fabian.* O, peace! now he's deeply in: look, how imagination blows him.

Malvolio. Having been three months married to her, sitting in my state—

(*Sir Toby*. O, for a stone-bow, to hit him in the eye!

Malvolio. Calling my officers about me, in my branched velvet gown; having come from a day-bed, where I have left Olivia sleeping—

50 (*Sir Toby*. Fire and brimstone!

(*Fabian*. O, peace, peace!

Malvolio. And then to have the humour of state: and after a demure travel of regard, telling them I know my place as I would they should do theirs, to ask for my kinsman Toby—

(*Sir Toby*. Bolts and shackles!

(*Fabian*. O, peace, peace, peace! now, now.

Malvolio. Seven of my people, with an obedient start, make out for him: I frown the while, and perchance wind

60 up my watch, or play with my [*touches his steward's chain an instant*]—some rich jewel...Toby approaches; curtsies there to me—

(*Sir Toby*. Shall this fellow live?

(*Fabian*. Though our silence be drawn from us with cars, yet peace.

Malvolio. I extend my hand to him thus; quenching my familiar smile with an austere regard of control—

(*Sir Toby*. And does not 'Toby' take you a blow o'the lips then?

70 *Malvolio*. Saying, 'Cousin Toby, my fortunes having cast me on your niece give me this prerogative of speech'—

Sir Toby. What, what?

Malvolio. 'You must amend your drunkenness.'

(*Sir Toby*. Out, scab!   [*Malvolio turns as at a sound*

(*Fabian*. Nay, patience, or we break the sinews of our plot.

Malvolio. 'Besides, you waste the treasure of your time with a foolish knight'—

(*Sir Andrew*. That's me, I warrant you.   80

Malvolio. 'One Sir Andrew'—   [*he sees the letter*

(*Sir Andrew*. I knew 'twas I, for many do call me fool.

Malvolio [*takes up the letter*]. What employment have we here?

(*Fabian*. Now is the woodcock near the gin.

(*Sir Toby*. O, peace! and the spirit of humours intimate reading aloud to him!

Malvolio. By my life, this is my lady's hand: these be her very *c*'s, her *u*'s, and her *t*'s, and thus makes 90 she her great *P*'s. It is, in contempt of question, her hand.

(*Sir Andrew*. Her *c*'s, her *u*'s, and her *t*'s: why that?

Malvolio [*reads the superscription*]. 'To the unknown beloved, this, and my good wishes'...her very phrases! By your leave, wax. Soft!—and the impressure her Lucrece, with which she uses to seal: 'tis my lady...To whom should this be?   [*he opens the letter*

(*Fabian*. This wins him, liver and all.

Malvolio [*reads*]. 'Jove knows I love: 100
                 But who?
             Lips, do not move!
             No man must know.'

'No man must know'....What follows? the numbers altered...[*he muses*] 'No man must know'—if this should be thee, Malvolio!

(*Sir Toby*. Marry, hang thee, brock!

Malvolio [*reads*].
         'I may command where I adore:
             But silence, like a Lucrece knife,
         With bloodless stroke my heart doth gore: 110
             M, O, A, I, doth sway my life.'

(*Fabian*. A fustian riddle!

⟨*Sir Toby*. Excellent wench, say I.

Malvolio. 'M, O, A, I, doth sway my life.'—Nay, but first, let me see, let me see, let me see.

⟨*Fabian*. What dish o' poison has she dressed him!

⟨*Sir Toby*. And with what wing the stallion checks at it!

Malvolio. 'I may command where I adore'...Why,
120 she may command me; I serve her, she is my lady....
Why, this is evident to any formal capacity. There is no obstruction in this. And the end: what should that alphabetical position portend? If I could make that resemble something in me! Softly! 'M, O, A, I,'—

⟨*Sir Toby*. O, ay, make up that—he is now at a cold scent.

⟨*Fabian*. Sowter will cry upon't for all this, though it be as rank as a fox.

Malvolio. 'M,'—Malvolio—'M,'—why, that begins
130 my name.

⟨*Fabian*. Did not I say he would work it out? the cur is excellent at faults.

Malvolio. 'M'—but then there is no consonancy in the sequel that suffers under probation: 'A' should follow, but 'O' does.

⟨*Fabian*. And O shall end, I hope.

⟨*Sir Toby*. Ay, or I'll cudgel him, and make him cry 'O!'

Malvolio. And then 'I' comes behind.
140 ⟨*Fabian*. Ay, an you had any eye behind you, you might see more detraction at your heels, than fortunes before you.

Malvolio. 'M, O, A, I.'...This simulation is not as the former: and yet, to crush this a little, it would bow to me, for every one of these letters are in my name. Soft! here follows prose....

[*reads*] 'If this fall into thy hand, revolve. In my stars I am above thee, but be not afraid of greatness: some are born great, some achieve greatness, and some have greatness thrust upon 'em. Thy Fates open their hands, let thy 150 blood and spirit embrace them; and to inure thyself to what thou art like to be, cast thy humble slough, and appear fresh. Be opposite with a kinsman, surly with servants; let thy tongue tang arguments of state; put thyself into the trick of singularity. She thus advises thee that sighs for thee. Remember who commended thy yellow stockings, and wished to see thee ever cross-gartered: I say, remember. Go to, thou art made, if thou desir'st to be so; if not, let me see thee a steward still, the fellow of servants, and not worthy to touch Fortune's 160 fingers. Farewell. She, that would alter services with thee,   THE FORTUNATE-UNHAPPY.'

Daylight and champian discovers not more: this is open. I will be proud, I will read politic authors, I will baffle Sir Toby, I will wash off gross acquaintance, I will be point-devise the very man. I do not now fool myself, to let imagination jade me; for every reason excites to this, that my lady loves me. She did commend my yellow stockings of late, she did praise my leg being cross- 170 gartered, and in this she manifests herself to my love, and with a kind of injunction drives me to these habits of her liking. I thank my stars, I am happy...I will be strange, stout, in yellow stockings, and cross-gartered, even with the swiftness of putting on. Jove, and my stars be praised! Here is yet a postscript.

[*reads*] 'Thou canst not choose but know who I am. If thou entertain'st my love, let it appear in thy smiling, thy smiles become thee well. Therefore in my presence still smile, dear, O my sweet, I prithee.'   180

Jove, I thank thee! [*he lifts his hands towards heaven*]
I will smile, I will do everything that thou wilt have me.
[*he goes within*

Fabian. I will not give my part of this sport for a
pension of thousands to be paid from the Sophy.

Sir Toby. I could marry this wench for this device—

Sir Andrew. So could I too.

Sir Toby. And ask no other dowry with her but such
another jest.

Sir Andrew. Nor I neither.

MARIA *comes from the house*

190 *Fabian.* Here comes my noble gull-catcher.

Sir Toby. Wilt thou set thy foot o' my neck?

Sir Andrew. Or o' mine either?

Sir Toby. Shall I play my freedom at trey-trip, and
become thy bond-slave?

Sir Andrew. I'faith or I either?

Sir Toby. Why, thou hast put him in such a dream,
that when the image of it leaves him he must run mad.

Maria. Nay, but say true, does it work upon him?

Sir Toby. Like aqua-vitæ with a midwife.

200 *Maria.* If you will then see the fruits of the sport, mark
his first approach before my lady: he will come to her in
yellow stockings, and 'tis a colour she abhors, and cross-
gartered, a fashion she detests; and he will smile upon
her, which will now be so unsuitable to her disposition,
being addicted to a melancholy as she is, that it cannot
but turn him into a notable contempt: if you will see it,
follow me.

Sir Toby. To the gates of Tartar, thou most excellent
devil of wit!

210 *Sir Andrew.* I'll make one too.   [*they enter the house*

[3. 1.] *The CLOWN enters the garden with his pipe and tabor; he plays. VIOLA comes in through the outer door as he finishes*

Viola. Save thee, friend, and thy music: dost thou live by thy tabor?

Clown. No, sir, I live by the church.

Viola. Art thou a churchman?

Clown. No such matter, sir, I do live by the church: for I do live at my house, and my house doth stand by the church.

Viola. So thou mayst say the king lies by a beggar, if a beggar dwell near him: or the church stands by thy tabor, if thy tabor stand by the church.   10

Clown. You have said, sir...To see this age! A sentence is but a cheveril glove to a good wit—how quickly the wrong side may be turned outward!

Viola. Nay, that's certain; they that dally nicely with words may quickly make them wanton.

Clown. I would therefore my sister had had no name, sir.

Viola. Why, man?

Clown. Why, sir, her name's a word, and to dally with that word might make my sister want-one...But indeed 20 words are very rascals since bonds disgraced them.

Viola. Thy reason, man?

Clown. Troth, sir, I can yield you none without words, and words are grown so false I am loath to prove reason with them.

Viola. I warrant thou art a merry fellow and car'st for nothing.

Clown. Not so, sir, I do care for something: but in my conscience, sir, I do not care for you: if that be to care for nothing, sir, I would it would make you invisible. 30

Viola. Art not thou the Lady Olivia's fool?

Clown. No indeed sir, the Lady Olivia has no folly. She will keep no fool, sir, till she be married, and fools are as like husbands as pilchards are to herrings—the husband's the bigger. I am, indeed, not her fool, but her corrupter of words.

Viola. I saw thee late at the Count Orsino's.

Clown. Foolery, sir, does walk about the orb like the sun, it shines every where. I would be sorry, sir, but the
40 fool should be as oft with your master as with my mistress: I think I saw your wisdom there.

Viola. Nay, an thou pass upon me, I'll no more with thee. Hold, there's expenses for thee.

[she gives him a coin

Clown [gazes at the coin in his palm]. Now Jove, in his next commodity of hair, send thee a beard!

Viola. By my troth I'll tell thee, I am almost sick for one—*[aside]* though I would not have it grow on my chin. Is thy lady within?

Clown [still gazes at the coin]. Would not a pair of
50 these have bred, sir?

Viola. Yes, being kept together and put to use.

Clown. I would play Lord Pandarus of Phrygia, sir, to bring a Cressida to this Troilus.

Viola. I understand you, sir, 'tis well begged.

[she gives another coin

Clown. The matter, I hope, is not great, sir; begging but a beggar: Cressida was a beggar. My lady is within, sir. I will conster to them whence you come, who you are and what you would are out of my welkin—I might say ' element,' but the word is over-worn. *[he goes within*
60 *Viola.* This fellow is wise enough to play the fool,
And to do that well craves a kind of wit:
He must observe their mood on whom he jests,

The quality of persons, and the time;
And, like the haggard, check at every feather
That comes before his eye. This is a practice,
As full of labour as a wise man's art:
For folly that he wisely shows is fit;
But wise men, folly-fall'n, quite taint their wit.

Sir TOBY BELCH and Sir ANDREW AGUECHEEK
come forth

Sir Toby. Save you, gentleman.
Viola. And you, sir.   70
Sir Andrew [*bows*]. Dieu vous garde, monsieur.
Viola [*bows*]. Et vous aussi; votre serviteur.
Sir Andrew. I hope, sir, you are—and I am yours.
Sir Toby. Will you encounter the house? my niece is
desirous you should enter, if your trade be to her.
Viola. I am bound to your niece, sir. I mean, she is
the list of my voyage.
Sir Toby. Taste your legs, sir, put them to motion.
Viola. My legs do better under-stand me, sir, than I
understand what you mean by bidding me taste my legs. 80
Sir Toby. I mean, to go, sir, to enter.
Viola. I will answer you with gate and entrance—but
we are prevented.

OLIVIA comes from the house with MARIA

Most excellent accomplished lady, the heavens rain
odours on you!
Sir Andrew. That youth's a rare courtier—'Rain
odours'—well!
Viola. My matter hath no voice, lady, but to your own
most pregnant and vouchsafed ear.
Sir Andrew. 'Odours,' 'pregnant,' and 'vouchsafed': 90
I'll get 'em all three all ready.

Olivia. Let the garden door be shut, and leave me to my hearing....

                  [Sir Toby, Sir Andrew and Maria depart

Give me your hand, sir.

Viola [bows low]. My duty, madam, and most humble service.

Olivia. What is your name?

Viola. Cesario is your servant's name, fair princess.

Olivia. My servant, sir! 'Twas never merry world,
100 Since lowly feigning was called compliment:
Y'are servant to the Count Orsino, youth.

Viola. And he is yours, and his must needs be yours;
Your servant's servant is your servant, madam.

Olivia. For him, I think not on him: for his thoughts,
Would they were blanks, rather than filled with me!

Viola. Madam, I come to whet your gentle thoughts
On his behalf.

Olivia.   O, by your leave, I pray you;
I bade you never speak again of him:
But, would you undertake another suit,
110 I had rather hear you to solicit that
Than music from the spheres.

Viola.   Dear lady,—

Olivia. Give me leave, beseech you: I did send,
After the last enchantment you did here,
A ring in chase of you; so did I abuse
Myself, my servant and, I fear me, you:
Under your hard construction must I sit,
To force that on you in a shameful cunning
Which you knew none of yours: what might you think?
Have you not set mine honour at the stake,
120 And baited it with all th'unmuzzled thoughts
That tyrannous heart can think?
To one of your receiving enough is shown,

A cypress, not a bosom, hides my heart:
So let me hear you speak.

  Viola.   I pity you.

  Olivia. That's a degree to love.

  Viola.   No, not a grise;
For 'tis a vulgar proof,
That very oft we pity enemies.

  Olivia. Why then methinks 'tis time to smile again:
O world, how apt the poor are to be proud!
If one should be a prey, how much the better   130
To fall before the lion than the wolf?   ['*clock strikes*'
The clock upbraids me with the waste of time...
Be not afraid, good youth, I will not have you:
And yet, when wit and youth is come to harvest,
Your wife is like to reap a proper man:
There lies your way, due west.

  Viola.   Then westward-ho!
Grace and good disposition attend your ladyship!
You'll nothing, madam, to my lord by me?

  Olivia. Stay:
I prithee, tell me what thou think'st of me.   140

  Viola. That you do think you are not what you are.

  Olivia. If I think so, I think the same of you.

  Viola. Then think you right; I am not what I am.

  Olivia. I would you were as I would have you be!

  Viola. Would it be better, madam, than I am,
I wish it might, for now I am your fool.

  Olivia. O, what a deal of scorn looks beautiful
In the contempt and anger of his lip!
A murd'rous guilt shows not itself more soon
Than love that would seem hid: love's night is noon.   150
Cesario, by the roses of the spring,
By maidhood, honour, truth, and every thing,
I love thee so, that, maugre all thy pride,

Nor wit nor reason can my passion hide.
Do not extort thy reasons from this clause,
For that I woo, thou therefore hast no cause:
But rather reason thus with reason fetter,
Love sought is good...but given unsought is better.

Viola. By innocence I swear, and by my youth,
160 I have one heart, one bosom, and one truth,
And that no woman has, nor never none
Shall mistress be of it, save I alone.
And so adieu, good madam! never more
Will I my master's tears to you deplore.

Olivia. Yet come again: for thou perhaps mayst move
That heart, which now abhors, to like his love.

[*they go*

[3. 2.]   *A room in Olivia's house*

Sir TOBY BELCH, Sir ANDREW AGUECHEEK,
and FABIAN

Sir Andrew. No, faith, I'll not stay a jot longer.

Sir Toby. Thy reason, dear venom, give thy reason.

Fabian. You must needs yield your reason, Sir
Andrew.

Sir Andrew. Marry, I saw your niece do more favours
to the count's serving-man than ever she bestowed upon
me; I saw't i'th'orchard.

Sir Toby. Did she see thee the while, old boy? tell me
that.

10 *Sir Andrew.* As plain as I see you now.

Fabian. This was a great argument of love in her
toward you.

Sir Andrew. 'Slight! will you make an ass o' me?

Fabian. I will prove it legitimate, sir, upon the oaths
of judgement and reason.

Sir Toby. And they have been grand-jurymen since before Noah was a sailor.

Fabian. She did show favour to the youth in your sight, only to exasperate you, to awake your dormouse valour, to put fire in your heart, and brimstone in your 20 liver: you should then have accosted her, and with some excellent jests, fire-new from the mint, you should have banged the youth into dumbness: this was looked for at your hand, and this was balked: the double gilt of this opportunity you let time wash off, and you are now sailed into the north of my lady's opinion, where you will hang like an icicle on a Dutchman's beard, unless you do redeem it by some laudable attempt, either of valour or policy.

Sir Andrew. An't be any way, it must be with valour, for 30 policy I hate: I had as lief be a Brownist, as a politician.

Sir Toby. Why then, build me thy fortunes upon the basis of valour. Challenge me the count's youth to fight with him, hurt him in eleven places—my niece shall take note of it, and assure thyself there is no love-broker in the world can more prevail in man's commendation with woman than report of valour.

Fabian. There is no way but this, Sir Andrew.

Sir Andrew. Will either of you bear me a challenge to him? 40

Sir Toby. Go, write it in a martial hand, be curst and brief; it is no matter how witty, so it be eloquent and full of invention: taunt him with the license of ink: if thou 'thou'st' him some thrice, it shall not be amiss; and as many lies as will lie in thy sheet of paper, although the sheet were big enough for the bed of Ware in England, set 'em down—go, about it. Let there be gall enough in thy ink, though thou write with a goose-pen, no matter: about it.

50 *Sir Andrew.* Where shall I find you?

Sir Toby. We'll call thee at thy †cubicle: go.

[*Sir Andrew goes*

Fabian. This is a dear manakin to you, Sir Toby.

Sir Toby. I have been dear to him, lad—some two thousand strong, or so.

Fabian. We shall have a rare letter from him...but you'll not deliver't?

Sir Toby. Never trust me then; and by all means stir on the youth to an answer. I think oxen and wainropes cannot hale them together. For Andrew, if he were 60 opened and you find so much blood in his liver as will clog the foot of a flea, I'll eat the rest of th'anatomy.

Fabian. And his opposite, the youth, bears in his visage no great presage of cruelty.

*MARIA comes tripping in, holding
her sides for laughter*

Sir Toby. Look, where the youngest wren of nine comes.

Maria. If you desire the spleen, and will laugh your-selves into stitches, follow me...Yon gull Malvolio is turned heathen, a very renegado; for there is no Christian, that means to be saved by believing rightly, 70 can ever believe such impossible passages of grossness....
[*overcome with laughter*] He's in yellow stockings!

Sir Toby [*shouts*]. And cross-gartered?

Maria. Most villainously; like a pedant that keeps a school i'th' church...I have dogged him like his murderer. He does obey every point of the letter that I dropped to betray him: he does smile his face into more lines than is in the new map, with the augmentation of the Indies: you have not seen such a thing as 'tis...I can hardly forbear hurling things at him, I know my lady

will strike him: if she do, he'll smile and take't for a great 80
favour.

Sir Toby. Come, bring us, bring us where he is.

[*they rush forth*

[3.3.]   *A street*

ANTONIO *and* SEBASTIAN *approach*

Sebastian. I would not by my will have troubled you,
But since you make your pleasure of your pains,
I will no further chide you.

Antonio. I could not stay behind you: my desire,
More sharp than filéd steel, did spur me forth;
And not all love to see you, though so much
As might have drawn one to a longer voyage,
But jealousy what might befall your travel,
Being skilless in these parts; which to a stranger,
Unguided and unfriended, often prove   10
Rough and unhospitable: my willing love,
The rather by these arguments of fear,
Set forth in your pursuit.

Sebastian.   My kind Antonio,
I can no other answer make but thanks,
†And thanks, and ever thanks; and oft good turns
Are shuffled off with such uncurrent pay:
But, were my worth as is my conscience firm,
You should find better dealing...What's to do?
Shall we go see the relics of this town?

Antonio. To-morrow sir—best first go see your lodging. 20

Sebastian. I am not weary, and 'tis long to night:
I pray you, let us satisfy our eyes
With the memorials and the things of fame
That do renown this city.

Antonio.   Would you'ld pardon me;
I do not without danger walk these streets.

Once in a sea-fight 'gainst the count his galleys
I did some service, of such note indeed
That were I ta'en here it would scarce be answered.
  Sebastian. Belike you slew great number of his people.
30 *Antonio.* Th'offence is not of such a bloody nature,
Albeit the quality of the time and quarrel
Might well have given us bloody argument:
It might have since been answered in repaying
What we took from them, which for traffic's sake
Most of our city did: only myself stood out,
For which, if I be lapséd in this place,
I shall pay dear.
  Sebastian.   Do not then walk too open.
  Antonio. It doth not fit me...Hold, sir, here's my
        purse.   *[he gives it*
In the south suburbs, at the Elephant,
40 Is best to lodge: I will bespeak our diet,
Whiles you beguile the time and feed your knowledge
With viewing of the town; there shall you have me.
  Sebastian. Why I your purse?
  Antonio. Haply your eye shall light upon some toy
You have desire to purchase; and your store,
I think, is not for idle markets, sir.
  Sebastian. I'll be your purse-bearer, and leave you for
an hour.
  Antonio. To th'Elephant.
50 *Sebastian.* I do remember.
                [they go off in different directions

[3. 4.]   *Olivia's garden*

OLIVIA *enters musing, followed by* MARIA;
Olivia sits

Olivia. I have sent after him, he says he'll come;
How shall I feast him? what bestow of him?
For youth is bought more oft than begged or borrowed.
I speak too loud...
[*to Maria*] Where's Malvolio? he is sad and civil,
And suits well for a servant with my fortunes—
Where is Malvolio?

Maria. He's coming, madam; but in very strange
manner. He is, sure, possessed, madam.

Olivia. Why, what's the matter? does he rave?   10

Maria. No, madam, he does nothing but smile: your
ladyship were best to have some guard about you, if he
come, for sure the man is tainted in's wits.

Olivia. Go, call him hither....

MALVOLIO, *in yellow stockings and with awkward
gait, is seen coming down the walk*

                      I am as mad as he,
If sad and merry madness equal be.
How now, Malvolio?

Malvolio. Sweet lady, ho, ho.

Olivia. Smil'st thou?
I sent for thee upon a sad occasion.

Malvolio. Sad, lady? I could be sad: this does make 20
some obstruction in the blood, this cross-gartering—but
what of that? if it please the eye of one, it is with me as
the very true sonnet is: 'Please one and please all.'

Olivia. Why, how dost thou, man? what is the matter
with thee?

Malvolio. Not black in my mind, though yellow in my legs...It did come to his hands, and commands shall be executed. I think we do know the sweet Roman hand.

30 *Olivia.* Wilt thou go to bed, Malvolio?

Malvolio. To bed! ay, sweet-heart, and I'll come to thee.

Olivia. God comfort thee! Why dost thou smile so, and kiss thy hand so oft?

Maria. How do you, Malvolio?

Malvolio [*disdainful*]. At your request! yes, nightingales answer daws.

Maria. Why appear you with this ridiculous boldness before my lady?

40 *Malvolio* [*to Olivia*]. 'Be not afraid of greatness': 'twas well writ.

Olivia. What mean'st thou by that, Malvolio?

Malvolio. 'Some are born great,'—

Olivia. Ha?

Malvolio. 'Some achieve greatness,'—

Olivia. What say'st thou?

Malvolio. 'And some have greatness thrust upon them.'

Olivia. Heaven restore thee!

50 *Malvolio.* 'Remember, who commended thy yellow stockings'—

Olivia. Thy yellow stockings!

Malvolio. 'And wished to see thee cross-gartered.'

Olivia. Cross-gartered?

Malvolio. 'Go to, thou art made, if thou desir'st to be so'—

Olivia. Am I made?

Malvolio. 'If not, let me see thee a servant still.'

Olivia. Why, this is very midsummer madness.

A servant comes from the house

Servant. Madam, the young gentleman of the Count 60
Orsino's is returned—I could hardly entreat him back:
he attends your ladyship's pleasure.

Olivia. I'll come to him. [*the servant goes*] Good
Maria, let this fellow be looked to. Where's my cousin
Toby? let some of my people have a special care of
him, I would not have him miscarry for the half of my
dowry.   [*she enters the house followed by Maria*

Malvolio. O, ho! do you come near me now? no worse
man than Sir Toby to look to me! This concurs directly
with the letter—she sends him on purpose, that I may 70
appear stubborn to him; for she incites me to that in the
letter. 'Cast thy humble slough,' says she; 'be opposite
with a kinsman, surly with servants, let thy tongue tang
with arguments of state, put thyself into the trick of
singularity'; and consequently sets down the manner
how; as, a sad face, a reverend carriage, a slow tongue,
in the habit of some sir of note, and so forth. I have
limed her, but it is Jove's doing, and Jove make me
thankful! And when she went away now, 'Let this
fellow be looked to': fellow! not Malvolio, nor after 80
my degree, but 'fellow.' Why, every thing adheres
together, that no dram of a scruple, no scruple
of a scruple, no obstacle, no incredulous or unsafe
circumstance—what can be said?—nothing that can be,
can come between me and the full prospect of my hopes.
Well, Jove, not I, is the doer of this, and he is to be
thanked.

Maria returns with Sir Toby Belch and Fabian

Sir Toby. Which way is he, in the name of sanctity?
If all the devils of hell be drawn in little, and Legion
himself possessed him, yet I'll speak to him.   90

Fabian. Here he is, here he is…How is't with you, sir?

†*Sir Toby.* How is't with you, man?

Malvolio. Go off, I discard you; let me enjoy my private: go off.

Maria. Lo, how hollow the fiend speaks within him! did not I tell you? Sir Toby, my lady prays you to have a care of him.

Malvolio. Ah, ha! does she so!

Sir Toby. Go to, go to: peace, peace, we must deal
100 gently with him: let me alone. How do you, Malvolio? how is't with you? What, man! defy the devil: consider, he's an enemy to mankind.

Malvolio. Do you know what you say?

Maria. La you! an you speak ill of the devil, how he takes it at heart! Pray God, he be not bewitched!

Fabian. Carry his water to th'wise woman.

Maria. Marry, and it shall be done to-morrow morning, if I live. My lady would not lose him for more than I'll say.

110 *Malvolio.* How now, mistress!

Maria [*chokes*]. O Lord!

Sir Toby. Prithee, hold thy peace, this is not the way: do you not see you move him? let me alone with him.

Fabian. No way but gentleness, gently, gently: the fiend is rough, and will not be roughly used.

Sir Toby. Why, how now, my bawcock! how dost thou, chuck?

Malvolio. Sir!

Sir Toby. Ay, Biddy, come with me. What, man! 'tis
120 not for gravity to play at cherry-pit with Satan. Hang him, foul collier!

Maria. Get him to say his prayers, good Sir Toby, get him to pray.

Malvolio. My prayers, minx!

Maria. No, I warrant you, he will not hear of godliness.

Malvolio. Go, hang yourselves all! you are idle shallow things—I am not of your element—you shall know more hereafter.

       [he goes; they gaze after him in amazement

Sir Toby. Is't possible?   130

Fabian. If this were played upon a stage now, I could condemn it as an improbable fiction.

Sir Toby. His very genius hath taken the infection of the device, man.

Maria. Nay, pursue him now, lest the device take air and taint.

Fabian. Why, we shall make him mad indeed.

Maria. The house will be the quieter.

Sir Toby. Come, we'll have him in a dark room and bound. My niece is already in the belief that he's mad; 140 we may carry it thus, for our pleasure and his penance, till our very pastime, tired out of breath, prompt us to have mercy on him: at which time we will bring the device to the bar and crown thee for a finder of madmen...But see, but see.

Sir ANDREW AGUECHEEK comes forth,
a letter in his hand

Fabian. More matter for a May morning!

Sir Andrew. Here's the challenge, read it: I warrant there's vinegar and pepper in't.

Fabian. Is't so saucy?

Sir Andrew. Ay, is't! I warrant him: do but read.   150

Sir Toby. Give me. *[he reads]* 'Youth, whatsoever thou art, thou art but a scurvy fellow.'

Fabian. Good, and valiant.

Sir Toby. 'Wonder not, nor admire not in thy mind,

why I do call thee so, for I will show thee no reason for't.'

Fabian. A good note, that keeps you from the blow of the law.

Sir Toby. 'Thou com'st to the Lady Olivia, and in my
160 sight she uses thee kindly: but thou liest in thy throat, that is not the matter I challenge thee for.'

Fabian. Very brief, and to exceeding good sense—
[*aside*] less.

Sir Toby. 'I will waylay thee going home, where if it be thy chance to kill me,'—

Fabian. Good.

Sir Toby. 'Thou kill'st me like a rogue and a villain.'

Fabian. Still you keep o'th' windy side of the law: good.

170 *Sir Toby.* 'Fare thee well, and God have mercy upon one of our souls! He may have mercy upon mine, but my hope is better, and so look to thyself. Thy friend, as thou usest him, and thy sworn enemy,

ANDREW AGUECHEEK.'

If this letter move him not, his legs cannot: I'll give't him.

Maria. You may have very fit occasion for't: he is now in some commerce with my lady, and will by and by depart.

180 *Sir Toby.* Go, Sir Andrew; scout me for him at the corner of the orchard like a bum-baily: so soon as ever thou seest him, draw, and as thou draw'st, swear horrible; for it comes to pass oft that a terrible oath, with a swaggering accent sharply twanged off, gives manhood more approbation than ever proof itself would have earned him. Away!

Sir Andrew. Nay, let me alone for swearing.

[*he leaves the garden by the outer door*

Sir Toby. Now will not I deliver his letter: for the
behaviour of the young gentleman gives him out to be of
good capacity and breeding; his employment between 190
his lord and my niece confirms no less; therefore this
letter, being so excellently ignorant, will breed no terror
in the youth: he will find it comes from a clodpole. But,
sir, I will deliver his challenge by word of mouth; set
upon Aguecheek a notable report of valour; and drive
the gentleman, as I know his youth will aptly receive it,
into a most hideous opinion of his rage, skill, fury and
impetuosity. This will so fright them both, that they will
kill one another by the look, like cockatrices.

OLIVIA and VIOLA come from the house

Fabian. Here he comes with your niece—give them 200
way till he take leave, and presently after him.

Sir Toby. I will meditate the while upon some horrid
message for a challenge.

[*Sir Toby, Fabian and Maria go off into the garden*

Olivia. I have said too much unto a heart of stone,
And laid mine honour too unchary out:
There's something in me that reproves my fault;
But such a headstrong potent fault it is,
That it but mocks reproof.

Viola. With the same 'haviour that your passion bears
Goes on my master's grief.   210

Olivia. Here, wear this jewel for me, 'tis my picture;
Refuse it not, it hath no tongue to vex you:
And I beseech you come again to-morrow.
What shall you ask of me, that I'll deny,
That honour saved may upon asking give?

Viola. Nothing but this—your true love for my master.

Olivia. How with mine honour may I give him that
Which I have given to you?

Viola.   I will acquit you.

Olivia. Well, come again to-morrow: fare thee well.
220 A fiend, like thee, might bear my soul to hell.

   [*she goes within; Viola walks toward the outer gate*

   Sir TOBY BELCH and FABIAN come up

Sir Toby. Gentleman, God save thee.

Viola [*turns*]. And you, sir.

Sir Toby. That defence thou hast, betake thee to't: of
what nature the wrongs are thou hast done him, I know
not; but thy intercepter, full of despite, bloody as the
hunter, attends thee at the orchard-end: dismount thy
tuck, be yare in thy preparation, for thy assailant is
quick, skilful and deadly.

Viola. You mistake, sir. I am sure no man hath any
230 quarrel to me; my remembrance is very free and clear
from any image of offence done to any man.

Sir Toby. You'll find it otherwise, I assure you: therefore, if you hold your life at any price, betake you to
your guard; for your opposite hath in him what youth,
strength, skill and wrath can furnish man withal.

Viola. I pray you, sir, what is he?

Sir Toby. He is knight, dubbed with unhatched rapier
and on carpet consideration, but he is a devil in private
brawl: souls and bodies hath he divorced three, and his
240 incensement at this moment is so implacable, that satis-
faction can be none but by pangs of death and sepulchre...
Hob, nob, is his word; give't or take't.

Viola. I will return again into the house and desire
some conduct of the lady. I am no fighter. I have heard
of some kind of men that put quarrels purposely on others,
to taste their valour: belike this is a man of that quirk.

Sir Toby. Sir, no; his indignation derives itself out of
a very competent injury, therefore get you on and give

him his desire. Back you shall not to the house, unless
you undertake that with me which with as much safety 250
you might answer him: therefore on, or strip your sword
stark naked; for meddle you must, that's certain, or forswear to wear iron about you.

Viola. This is as uncivil as strange. I beseech you, do
me this courteous office, as to know of the knight what
my offence to him is; it is something of my negligence,
nothing of my purpose.

Sir Toby. I will do so. Signior Fabian, [*he winks*] stay
you by this gentleman till my return.

[*he departs by the outer door*

Viola. Pray you, sir, do you know of this matter?   260

Fabian. I know the knight is incensed against you,
even to a mortal arbitrement, but nothing of the
circumstance more.

Viola. I beseech you, what manner of man is he?

Fabian. Nothing of that wonderful promise, to read
him by his form, as you are like to find him in the proof
of his valour. He is indeed, sir, the most skilful, bloody
and fatal opposite that you could possibly have found in
any part of Illyria...[*he takes her by the arm*] Will you
walk towards him? I will make your peace with him 270
if I can.

Viola. I shall be much bound to you for't: I am one,
that had rather go with sir priest than sir knight: I care
not who knows so much of my mettle.

[*they leave the garden*

*A quiet street at the back of Olivia's walled garden,
with a gate leading thereto; trees and shrubs*

Sir Toby and Sir Andrew

Sir Toby. Why, man, he's a very devil, I have not
seen such a firago...I had a pass with him, rapier,

scabbard and all, and he gives me the stuck in with such
a mortal motion that it is inevitable; and on the answer,
he pays you as surely as your feet hit the ground they
280 step on. They say he has been fencer to the Sophy.

Sir Andrew. Pox on't, I'll not meddle with him.

Sir Toby. Ay, but he will not now be pacified: Fabian
can scarce hold him yonder.

Sir Andrew. Plague on't, an I thought he had been
valiant and so cunning in fence, I'd have seen him
damned ere I'd have challenged him. Let him let the
matter slip, and I'll give him my horse, grey Capilet.

Sir Toby. I'll make the motion: stand here, make a good
show on't—this shall end without the perdition of souls.
290 [*aside*] Marry, I'll ride your horse as well as I ride you

> *FABIAN and VIOLA come from the garden;*
> *Sir Toby beckons Fabian aside*

I have his horse to take up the quarrel; I have persuaded
him the youth's a devil.

(*Fabian.* He is as horribly conceited of him; and pants
and looks pale, as if a bear were at his heels.

Sir Toby [*to Viola*]. There's no remedy, sir, he will
fight with you for's oath sake: marry, he hath better be-
thought him of his quarrel, and he finds that now scarce
to be worth talking of: therefore draw for the sup-
portance of his vow, he protests he will not hurt you.

300 (*Viola.* Pray God defend me! A little thing would
make me tell them how much I lack of a man.

Fabian. Give ground, if you see him furious.

Sir Toby. Come, Sir Andrew, there's no remedy, the
gentleman will for his honour's sake have one bout with
you: he cannot by the duello avoid it: but he has promised
me, as he is a gentleman and a soldier, he will not hurt
you. Come on, to't!

Sir Andrew. Pray God, he keep his oath!
Viola. I do assure you, 'tis against my will.

They make ready to fight; ANTONIO comes up

Antonio [to Sir Andrew]. Put up your sword: if this
     young gentleman   310
Have done offence, I take the fault on me;
If you offend him, I for him defy you.

Sir Toby. You, sir! why, what are you?

Antonio. One, sir, that for his love dares yet do more
Than you have heard him brag to you he will.

Sir Toby. Nay, if you be an undertaker, I am for you.
                            [they draw

Two officers approach

Fabian. O good Sir Toby, hold; here come the
     officers.

Sir Toby [to Antonio]. I'll be with you anon.
          [he hides from the officers behind a tree

Viola [to Sir Andrew]. Pray, sir, put your sword up,
if you please.   320

Sir Andrew. Marry, will I, sir; and, for that I
promised you, I'll be as good as my word. *[he sheathes his
sword]* He will bear you easily, and reins well.

1 *Officer.* This is the man, do thy office.

2 *Officer.* Antonio, I arrest thee at the suit
Of Count Orsino.

Antonio.   You do mistake me, sir.

1 *Officer.* No, sir, no jot; I know your favour well:
Though now you have no sea-cap on your head...
Take him away, he knows I know him well.

Antonio. I must obey. *[to Viola]* This comes with
     seeking you;   330
But there's no remedy, I shall answer it...

What will you do, now my necessity
Makes me to ask you for my purse? it grieves me
Much more for what I cannot do for you
Than what befalls myself...You stand amazed,
But be of comfort.
   2 *Officer.* Come, sir, away.
   Antonio. I must entreat of you some of that money.
   Viola. What money, sir?
340 For the fair kindness you have showed me here,
And part being prompted by your present trouble,
Out of my lean and low ability
I'll lend you something...[*opens her purse*] My having
     is not much,
I'll make division of my present with you:
Hold, there's half my coffer.   [*she proffers coin*
   Antonio [*refuses it*].   Will you deny me now?
Is't possible that my deserts to you
Can lack persuasion? Do not tempt my misery,
Lest that it make me so unsound a man
As to upbraid you with those kindnesses
350 That I have done for you.
   Viola.   I know of none,
Nor know I you by voice or any feature:
I hate ingratitude more in a man,
Than lying vainness, babbling drunkenness,
Or any taint of vice whose strong corruption
Inhabits our frail blood.
   Antonio.   O heavens themselves!
   2 *Officer.* Come, sir, I pray you, go.
   Antonio.   Let me speak a little.
This youth that you see here
I snatched one half out of the jaws of death,
Relieved him with such sanctity of love,
360 And to his image, which methought did promise

Most venerable worth, did I devotion.

1 Officer. What's that to us? The time goes by: away!

Antonio. But, O, how vile an idol proves this god!
Thou hast, Sebastian, done good feature shame.
In nature there's no blemish but the mind;
None can be called deformed but the unkind:
Virtue is beauty, but the beauteous evil
Are empty trunks o'erflourished by the devil.

1 Officer. The man grows mad, away with him!
Come, come, sir.   370

Antonio. Lead me on.   [*they carry him off*

Viola. Methinks his words do from such passion fly,
That he believes himself—so do not I?
Prove true, imagination, O prove true,
That I, dear brother, be now ta'en for you!

Sir Toby [*peeps from behind the tree*]. Come hither,
knight—come hither, Fabian; we'll whisper o'er a
couplet or two of most sage saws.

Viola. He named Sebastian; I my brother know
Yet living in my glass; even such and so   380
In favour was my brother, and he went
Still in this fashion, colour, ornament,
For him I imitate: O, if it prove,
Tempests are kind and salt waves fresh in love!

                                              [*she goes*

Sir Toby. A very dishonest paltry boy, and more a
coward than a hare. His dishonesty appears in leaving
his friend here in necessity and denying him; and for his
cowardship, ask Fabian.

Fabian. A coward, a most devout coward, religious
in it.   390

Sir Andrew. 'Slid, I'll after him again and beat him.

Sir Toby. Do, cuff him soundly, but never draw thy
sword.

Sir Andrew. An I do not,—

    [*he draws his sword and hurries after Viola*
Fabian. Come, let's see the event.

Sir Toby. I dare lay any money, 'twill be nothing yet.

        [*they follow Sir Andrew*

[4. 1.]   *A square before* Olivia's *house*

SEBASTIAN *and* CLOWN

Clown. Will you make me believe that I am not sent
for you?

Sebastian. Go to, go to, thou art a foolish fellow;
Let me be clear of thee.

Clown. Well held out, i'faith! No, I do not know you,
nor I am not sent to you by my lady to bid you come
speak with her, nor your name is not Master Cesario,
nor this is not my nose neither: nothing that is so, is so.

Sebastian. I prithee, vent thy folly somewhere else,
10 Thou know'st not me.

Clown. Vent my folly! He has heard that word of some
great man and now applies it to a fool. Vent my folly!
I am afraid this great lubber, the world, will prove a
cockney...I prithee now, ungird thy strangeness and
tell me what I shall vent to my lady: [*whispers, winking*]
shall I vent to her that thou art coming?

Sebastian. I prithee, foolish Greek, depart from me.
There's money for thee [*he gives a coin*]—if you tarry
   longer
I shall give worse payment.

20 *Clown.* By my troth, thou hast an open hand...These
wise men that give fools money get themselves a good
report—after fourteen years' purchase.

Sir ANDREW *with drawn sword enters the square,*
Sir TOBY *and* FABIAN *following*

Sir Andrew. Now, sir, have I met you again? there's
for you. *[he strikes wide*

Sebastian [replies with his fists]. Why, there's for thee,
and there, and there! *[he knocks him down*
Are all the people mad? *[his hand upon his dagger*

Sir Toby [seizes him from behind]. Hold, sir, or I'll
throw your dagger o'er the house.

Clown. This will I tell my lady straight: I would not
be in some of your coats for two pence. *[he goes within* 30

Sir Toby. Come on, sir! hold! *[Sebastian struggles*

Sir Andrew [rubbing his bruises]. Nay, let him alone,
I'll go another way to work with him: I'll have an action
of battery against him, if there be any law in Illyria:
though I struck him first, yet it's no matter for that.

Sebastian. Let go thy hand!

Sir Toby. Come, sir, I will not let you go. *[to Sir*
Andrew] Come, my young soldier, put up your iron:
you are well fleshed...*[to Sebastian]* Come on.

Sebastian. I will be free from thee....*[he throws him*
off] What wouldst thou now? *[he draws* 40
If thou dar'st tempt me further, draw thy sword.

Sir Toby. What, what? *[he also draws]* Nay, then I
must have an ounce or two of this malapert blood from
you. *[they begin to fight*

OLIVIA *comes from the house*

Olivia. Hold, Toby! on thy life, I charge thee, hold!
Sir Toby. Madam! *[they break off*
Olivia. Will it be ever thus? Ungracious wretch,
Fit for the mountains and the barbarous caves,
Where manners ne'er were preached! out of my sight!

50 Be not offended, dear Cesario...
   Rudesby, be gone!
               [*Sir Toby, Sir Andrew and Fabian slink off*
                  I prithee, gentle friend,
   Let thy fair wisdom, not thy passion, sway
   In this uncivil and unjust extent
   Against thy peace. Go with me to my house,
   And hear thou there how many fruitless pranks
   This ruffian hath botched up, that thou thereby
   Mayst smile at this...[*he draws back*] Thou shalt not
       choose but go;
   Do not deny. Beshrew his soul for me,
   He started one poor heart of mine in thee.
60 (*Sebastian.* What relish is in this? how runs the stream?
   Or I am mad, or else this is a dream:
   Let fancy still my sense in Lethe steep—
   If it be thus to dream, still let me sleep!
   Olivia. Nay, come, I prithee: would thou'dst be
      ruled by me!
   Sebastian. Madam, I will.
   Olivia.   O, say so, and so be!
                       [*they go in*

[4. 2.] *A room in Olivia's house; at the back a closet*
       with a curtain before it

   C*LOWN and* MARIA, *holding a black gown and*
       a false beard in her hand

Maria. Nay, I prithee, put on this gown and this
beard, make him believe thou art Sir Topas the curate,
do it quickly. I'll call Sir Toby the whilst. [*she goes out*
   Clown. Well, I'll put it on, and I will dissemble myself
in't, and I would I were the first that ever dissembled in
such a gown. [*he dons the gown and the beard*] I am not
tall enough to become the function well, nor lean

enough to be thought a good student: but to be said an honest man and a good housekeeper goes as fairly as to say a careful man and a great scholar. The competitors 10 enter.

MARIA returns with Sir TOBY

Sir Toby. Jove bless thee, Master Parson!

Clown [*in feigned voice*]. Bonos dies, Sir Toby: for as the old hermit of Prague, that never saw pen and ink, very wittily said to a niece of King Gorboduc, 'That that is, is': so I, being Master Parson, am Master Parson; for what is 'that' but that? and 'is' but is?

Sir Toby. To him, Sir Topas.

Clown [*draws near the curtain*]. What, ho, I say! peace in this prison!   20

(*Sir Toby.* The knave counterfeits well; a good knave.

Malvolio [*from the closet*]. Who calls there?

Clown. Sir Topas the curate, who comes to visit Malvolio the lunatic.

Malvolio. Sir Topas, Sir Topas, good Sir Topas, go to my lady.

Clown. Out, hyperbolical fiend! how vexest thou this man? talkest thou nothing but of ladies?

Sir Toby. Well said, Master Parson.

Malvolio. Sir Topas, never was man thus wronged— 30 good Sir Topas, do not think I am mad; they have laid me here in hideous darkness.

Clown. Fie, thou dishonest Satan! I call thee by the most modest terms, for I am one of those gentle ones that will use the devil himself with courtesy: say'st thou that house is dark?

Malvolio. As hell, Sir Topas.

Clown. Why, it hath bay windows transparent as barricadoes, and the clerestories toward the south-north

40 are as lustrous as ebony; and yet complainest thou of
obstruction?

Malvolio. I am not mad, Sir Topas. I say to you, this
house is dark.

Clown. Madman, thou errest: I say, there is no darkness but ignorance, in which thou art more puzzled than
the Egyptians in their fog.

Malvolio. I say, this house is as dark as ignorance,
though ignorance were as dark as hell; and I say, there
was never man thus abused. I am no more mad than
50 you are—make the trial of it in any constant question.

Clown. What is the opinion of Pythagoras concerning
wild fowl?

Malvolio. That the soul of our grandam might haply
inhabit a bird.

Clown. What think'st thou of his opinion?

Malvolio. I think nobly of the soul, and no way
approve his opinion.

Clown. Fare thee well: remain thou still in darkness.
Thou shalt hold th'opinion of Pythagoras ere I will
60 allow of thy wits, and fear to kill a woodcock, lest thou
dispossess the soul of thy grandam. Fare thee well.

　　　　　　　[he turns back from before the curtain

Malvolio [calls]. Sir Topas, Sir Topas!

Sir Toby. My most exquisite Sir Topas!

Clown. Nay, I am for all waters.

　　　　　　　　　　[he puts off the disguise

Maria. Thou mightst have done this without thy
beard and gown, he sees thee not.

Sir Toby. To him in thine own voice, and bring me
word how thou find'st him...[*to Maria*] I would we
were well rid of this knavery. If he may be conveniently
70 delivered, I would he were, for I am now so far in
offence with my niece, that I cannot pursue with any

safety this sport to the upshot. Come by and by to my chamber. [*Sir Toby and Maria go out by different doors*

Clown [*sings*]. 'Hey Robin, jolly Robin,

                Tell me how thy lady does.'

Malvolio. Fool,—

Clown [*sings*]. 'My lady is unkind, perdy.'

Malvolio. Fool,—

Clown [*sings*]. 'Alas, why is she so?'

Malvolio. Fool, I say,—   80

Clown [*sings*]. 'She loves another'—Who calls, ha?

Malvolio. Good fool, as ever thou wilt deserve well at my hand, help me to a candle, and pen, ink and paper; as I am a gentleman, I will live to be thankful to thee for't.

Clown. Master Malvolio!

Malvolio. Ay, good fool.

Clown. Alas, sir, how fell you besides your five wits?

Malvolio. Fool, there was never man so notoriously abused: I am as well in my wits, fool, as thou art.

Clown. But as well? then you are mad indeed, if you 90 be no better in your wits than a fool.

Malvolio. They have here propertied me; keep me in darkness, send ministers to me, asses, and do all they can to face me out of my wits.

Clown. Advise you what you say; the minister is here....[*he changes his voice*] Malvolio, Malvolio, thy wits the heavens restore! endeavour thyself to sleep, and leave thy vain bibble babble.

Malvolio. Sir Topas,—

Clown. Maintain no words with him, good fellow.— 100 Who, I, sir? not I, sir. God buy you, good Sir Topas.— Marry, amen.—I will, sir, I will.

Malvolio. Fool, fool, fool, I say,—

Clown. Alas, sir, be patient. What say you, sir? I am shent for speaking to you.

Malvolio. Good fool, help me to some light and some paper. I tell thee, I am as well in my wits, as any man in Illyria.

Clown. Well-a-day that you were, sir!

110 *Malvolio.* By this hand, I am...Good fool, some ink, paper and light: and convey what I will set down to my lady; it shall advantage thee more than ever the bearing of letter did.

Clown. I will help you to't. But tell me true, are you not mad indeed? or do you but counterfeit?

Malvolio. Believe me, I am not—I tell thee true.

Clown. Nay, I'll ne'er believe a madman till I see his brains. I will fetch you light and paper and ink.

Malvolio. Fool, I'll requite it in the highest degree:
120 I prithee, be gone.

Clown [*sings as he dances from the room*].

> I am gone, sir, and anon, sir,
> I'll be with you again:
>   In a trice, like to the old Vice,
> Your need to sustain.
> Who with dagger of lath,
> In his rage and his wrath,
>   Cries ah ha, to the devil:
> Like a mad lad,
> Pare thy nails dad,

130 >   Adieu goodman devil.   [*he goes*

[4. 3.]   *Olivia's garden*

SEBASTIAN *comes from the house*

Sebastian. This is the air, that is the glorious sun,
This pearl she gave me, I do feel't and see't,
And though 'tis wonder that enwraps me thus,
Yet 'tis not madness. Where's Antonio then?

I could not find him at the Elephant,
Yet there he was, and there I found this credit,
That he did range the town to seek me out.
His counsel now might do me golden service,
For though my soul disputes well with my sense,
That this may be some error, but no madness, 10
Yet doth this accident and flood of fortune
So far exceed all instance, all discourse,
That I am ready to distrust mine eyes
And wrangle with my reason, that persuades me
To any other trust but that I am mad,
Or else the lady's mad; yet, if 'twere so,
She could not sway her house, command
      her followers,
Take and give back affairs and their dispatch,
With such a smooth, discreet, and stable bearing
As I perceive she does: there's something in't 20
That is deceivable. But here the lady comes.

OLIVIA comes forth with a priest

Olivia. Blame not this haste of mine…If you
      mean well,
Now go with me and with this holy man
Into the chantry by: there, before him,
And underneath that consecrated roof,
Plight me the full assurance of your faith,
That my most jealous and too doubtful soul
May live at peace. He shall conceal it,
Whiles you are willing it shall come to note,
What time we will our celebration keep 30
According to my birth. What do you say?
  Sebastian. I'll follow this good man and go
      with you,
And having sworn truth, ever will be true.

Olivia. Then lead the way, good father, and heavens
    so shine,
That they may fairly note this act of mine!   [*they go*

[5. 1.]   *The square before Olivia's house*

CLOWN *and* FABIAN

Fabian. Now, as thou lov'st me, let me see his letter.

Clown. Good Master Fabian, grant me another
request.

Fabian. Any thing.

Clown. Do not desire to see this letter.

Fabian. This is, to give a dog, and in recompense
desire my dog again.

The DUKE *and* VIOLA (*as* Cesario) *enter the square with attendants*

Duke. Belong you to the Lady Olivia, friends?

Clown. Ay, sir, we are some of her trappings.

10 *Duke.* I know thee well: how dost thou, my good
fellow?

Clown. Truly, sir, the better for my foes and the worse
for my friends.

Duke. Just the contrary; the better for thy friends.

Clown. No, sir, the worse.

Duke. How can that be?

Clown. Marry, sir, they praise me and make an ass
of me; now my foes tell me plainly I am an ass: so that
by my foes, sir, I profit in the knowledge of myself, and
20 by my friends I am abused: so that, conclusions to be as
kisses, if your four negatives make your two affirmatives,
why then—the worse for my friends and the better for
my foes.

Duke. Why, this is excellent.

Clown. By my troth, sir, no; though it please you to be one of my friends.

Duke. Thou shalt not be the worse for me—there's gold.   [*he gives him money*

Clown. But that it would be double-dealing, sir, I would you could make it another.   30

Duke. O, you give me ill counsel.

Clown. Put your grace in your pocket, sir, for this once, and let your flesh and blood obey it.

Duke. Well, I will be so much a sinner, to be a double-dealer; there's another.   [*he gives more money*

Clown. Primo, secundo, tertio, is a good play, and the old saying is, the third pays for all: the triplex, sir, is a good tripping measure, or the bells of St Bennet, sir, may put you in mind—one, two, three!

Duke. You can fool no more money out of me at this   40
throw: if you will let your lady know I am here to speak with her, and bring her along with you, it may awake my bounty further.

Clown. Marry, sir, lullaby to your bounty till I come again. I go, sir, but I would not have you to think that my desire of having is the sin of covetousness: but, as you say, sir, let your bounty take a nap, I will awake it anon.   [*he goes within*

Officers approach with ANTONIO *bound*

Viola. Here comes the man, sir, that did rescue me.

Duke. That face of his I do remember well,   50
Yet when I saw it last it was besmeared
As black as Vulcan in the smoke of war:
A baubling vessel was he captain of,
For shallow draught and bulk unprizable,
With which such scathful grapple did he make

With the most noble bottom of our fleet,
That very envy and the tongue of loss
Cried fame and honour on him. What's the matter?
    1 *Officer.* Orsino, this is that Antonio
60 That took the Phœnix and her fraught from Candy,
And this is he that did the Tiger board,
When your young nephew Titus lost his leg:
Here in the streets, desperate of shame and state,
In private brabble did we apprehend him.
    Viola. He did me kindness, sir, drew on my side,
But in conclusion put strange speech upon me,
I know not what 'twas but distraction.
    Duke. Notable pirate! thou salt-water thief!
What foolish boldness brought thee to their mercies,
70 Whom thou, in terms so bloody and so dear,
Hast made thine enemies?
    Antonio.   Orsino, noble sir,
Be pleased that I shake off these names you give me;
Antonio never yet was thief or pirate,
Though I confess, on base and ground enough,
Orsino's enemy. A witchcraft drew me hither:
That most ingrateful boy there by your side,
From the rude sea's enraged and foamy mouth
Did I redeem; a wrack past hope he was:
His life I gave him and did thereto add
80 My love, without retention or restraint,
All his in dedication. For his sake
Did I expose myself—pure for his love!—
Into the danger of this adverse town,
Drew to defend him when he was beset:
Where being apprehended, his false cunning,
Not meaning to partake with me in danger,
Taught him to face me out of his acquaintance,
And grew a twenty years removéd thing

While one would wink; denied me mine own purse,
Which I had recommended to his use   90
Not half an hour before.
    Viola.   How can this be?
    Duke. When came he to this town?
    Antonio. To-day, my lord; and for three
        months before,
No interim, not a minute's vacancy,
Both day and night did we keep company.

    OLIVIA comes from her house, attended

    Duke. Here comes the countess! now heaven walks
        on earth...
But for thee, fellow—fellow, thy words are madness,
Three months this youth hath tended upon me.
But more of that anon....Take him aside.
                        [*the officers obey*
    Olivia [*draws near*]. What would my lord, but that
        he may not have,   100
Wherein Olivia may seem serviceable?
Cesario, you do not keep promise with me.
    Viola. Madam?
    Duke. Gracious Olivia,—
    Olivia. What do you say, Cesario?—Good my lord,—
    Viola. My lord would speak, my duty hushes me.
    Olivia. If it be aught to the old tune, my lord,
It is as fat and fulsome to mine ear
As howling after music.
    Duke.   Still so cruel?
    Olivia. Still so constant, lord.   110
    Duke. What, to perverseness? you uncivil lady,
To whose ingrate and unauspicious altars
My soul the faithfull'st off'rings hath breathed out,
That e'er devotion tendered! What shall I do?

Olivia. Even what it please my lord, that shall
    become him.
  Duke. Why should I not, had I the heart to do it,
Like to th'Egyptian thief, at point of death,
Kill what I love?—a savage jealousy
That sometime savours nobly. But hear me this:
120 Since you to non-regardance cast my faith,
And that I partly know the instrument
That screws me from my true place in your favour,
Live you, the marble-breasted tyrant, still;
But this your minion, whom I know you love,
And whom, by heaven I swear, I tender dearly,
Him will I tear out of that cruel eye,
Where he sits crownéd in his master's spite....
Come boy with me. My thoughts are ripe in mischief:
I'll sacrifice the lamb that I do love,
130 To spite a raven's heart within a dove. [*he turns away
    Viola* [*follows*]. And I, most jocund, apt and willingly,
To do you rest, a thousand deaths would die.
  Olivia. Where goes Cesario?
  Viola.   After him I love
More than I love these eyes, more than my life,
More, by all mores, than e'er I shall love wife.
If I do feign, you witnesses above
Punish my life for tainting of my love!
  Olivia. Ay me, detested! how am I beguiled!
  Viola. Who does beguile you? who does do
    you wrong?
140 *Olivia.* Hast thou forgot thyself? is it so long?
Call forth the holy father. [*an attendant goes within
  Duke [*to Viola*].   Come, away!
  Olivia. Whither, my lord? Cesario, husband, stay.
  Duke. Husband?
  Olivia.   Ay, husband. Can he that deny?

Duke. Her husband, sirrah?
Viola.   No, my lord, not I.
Olivia. Alas, it is the baseness of thy fear,
That makes thee strangle thy propriety:
Fear not, Cesario, take thy fortunes up,
Be that thou know'st thou art, and then thou art
As great as that thou fear'st.

The priest comes forth

                    O, welcome, father!
Father, I charge thee, by thy reverence,   150
Here to unfold—though lately we intended
To keep in darkness, what occasion now
Reveals before 'tis ripe—what thou dost know
Hath newly passed between this youth and me.
Priest. A contract of eternal bond of love,
Confirmed by mutual joinder of your hands,
Attested by the holy close of lips,
Strength'ned by interchangement of your rings,
And all the ceremony of this compact
Sealed in my function, by my testimony: 160
Since when, my watch hath told me, toward my grave,
I have travelled but two hours.
Duke. O, thou dissembling cub! what wilt thou be
When time hath sowed a grizzle on thy case?
Or will not else thy craft so quickly grow,
That thine own trip shall be thine overthrow?
Farewell, and take her, but direct thy feet
Where thou and I henceforth may never meet.
Viola. My lord, I do protest—
Olivia.   O, do not swear!
Hold little faith, though thou hast too much fear.   170

*Sir ANDREW AGUECHEEK comes up
with his head broke*

Sir Andrew. For the love of God, a surgeon! Send one
presently to Sir Toby.

Olivia. What's the matter?

Sir Andrew. H'as broke my head across and has given
Sir Toby a bloody coxcomb too: for the love of God,
your help! I had rather than forty pound I were at home.

[he sinks to the ground

Olivia. Who has done this, Sir Andrew?

Sir Andrew. The count's gentleman, one Cesario: we
took him for a coward, but he's the very devil incardi-
180 nate.

Duke. My gentleman, Cesario?

Sir Andrew. 'Od's lifelings, here he is! You broke
my head for nothing, and that that I did, I was set on to
do't by Sir Toby.

Viola. Why do you speak to me? I never hurt you:
You drew your sword upon me without cause,
But I bespake you fair, and hurt you not.

Sir Andrew. If a bloody coxcomb be a hurt, you have
hurt me; I think you set nothing by a bloody coxcomb.

Sir TOBY approaches bleeding, led by the CLOWN

190 Here comes Sir Toby halting, you shall hear more: but
if he had not been in drink, he would have tickled you
othergates than he did.

Duke. How now, gentleman! how is't with you?

Sir Toby. That's all one—has hurt me, and there's
th'end on't...[*to Clown*] Sot, didst see Dick surgeon,
sot?

Clown. O he's drunk, Sir Toby, an hour agone; his
eyes were set at eight i'th' morning.

Sir Toby. Then he's a rogue, and a passy-measures
pavin: I hate a drunken rogue.   200

Olivia. Away with him! Who hath made this havoc
with them?

Sir Andrew [*rises*]. I'll help you, Sir Toby, because
we'll be dressed together.

Sir Toby. Will you help? an ass-head, and a coxcomb,
and a knave! a thin-faced knave, a gull!

Olivia. Get him to bed, and let his hurt be looked to.
        [*Clown, Sir Toby, and Sir Andrew go within*

                SEBASTIAN *enters the square*

Sebastian. I am sorry, madam, I have hurt
        your kinsman;
But, had it been the brother of my blood,
I must have done no less with wit and safety.   210
                        [*all stand in amaze*
You throw a strange regard upon me, and by that
I do perceive it hath offended you;
Pardon me, sweet one, even for the vows
We made each other but so late ago.

Duke. One face, one voice, one habit, and
        two persons,
A natural perspective, that is and is not.

Sebastian. Antonio! O my dear Antonio!
How have the hours racked and tortured me,
Since I have lost thee!

Antonio. Sebastian are you?

Sebastian.   Fear'st thou that, Antonio? 220

Antonio. How have you made division of yourself?
An apple, cleft in two, is not more twin
Than these two creatures. Which is Sebastian?

Olivia. Most wonderful!

Sebastian. Do I stand there? I never had a brother:

Nor can there be that deity in my nature,
Of here and every where. I had a sister,
Whom the blind waves and surges have devoured...
Of charity, what kin are you to me?
230 What countryman? what name? what parentage?
   Viola. Of Messaline: Sebastian was my father—
Such a Sebastian was my brother too:
So went he suited to his watery tomb:
If spirits can assume both form and suit,
You come to fright us.
   Sebastian.   A spirit I am indeed,
But am in that dimension grossly clad,
Which from the womb I did participate.
Were you a woman, as the rest goes even,
I should my tears let fall upon your cheek,
240 And say 'Thrice-welcome, drownéd Viola!'
   Viola. My father had a mole upon his brow.
   Sebastian. And so had mine.
   Viola. And died that day when Viola from
        her birth
Had numb'red thirteen years.
   Sebastian. O, that record is lively in my soul!
He finishéd indeed his mortal act,
That day that made my sister thirteen years.
   Viola. If nothing lets to make us happy both,
But this my masculine usurped attire,
250 Do not embrace me till each circumstance
Of place, time, fortune, do cohere and jump
That I am Viola—which to confirm,
I'll bring you to a captain in this town,
Where lie my maiden weeds; by whose gentle help
I was preserved to serve this noble count...
All the occurrence of my fortune since
Hath been between this lady and this lord.

Sebastian [*to Olivia*]. So comes it, lady, you have
        been mistook;
But nature to her bias drew in that.
You would have been contracted to a maid,   260
Nor are you therein, by my life, deceived,
You are betrothed both to a maid and man.
  Duke. Be not amazed—right noble is his blood...
If this be so, as yet the glass seems true,
I shall have share in this most happy wrack.
[*to Viola*] Boy, thou hast said to me a thousand times
Thou never shouldst love woman like to me.
  Viola. And all those sayings will I over-swear,
And all those swearings keep as true in soul,
As doth that orbéd continent the fire   270
That severs day from night.
  Duke.   Give me thy hand,
And let me see thee in thy woman's weeds.
  Viola. The captain that did bring me first on shore,
Hath my maid's garments: he upon some action
Is now in durance, at Malvolio's suit,
A gentleman and follower of my lady's.
  Olivia. He shall enlarge him...Fetch Malvolio
        hither—
And yet, alas, now I remember me,
They say, poor gentleman, he's much distract.

        The CLOWN *returns with a letter in his hand,*
                FABIAN *following*

A most extracting frenzy of mine own   280
From my remembrance clearly banished his.
How does he, sirrah?
  Clown. Truly, madam, he holds Belzebub at the
stave's end as well as a man in his case may do: has here
writ a letter to you, I should have given't you to-day

morning: but as a madman's epistles are no gospels, so
it skills not much when they are delivered.

Olivia. Open't, and read it.

Clown. Look then to be well edified, when the fool
290 delivers the madman. [*he shrieks*] 'By the Lord,
madam,'—

Olivia. How now! art thou mad?

Clown. No, madam, I do but read madness: an your
ladyship will have it as it ought to be, you must allow
Vox.

Olivia. Prithee, read i'thy right wits.

Clown. So I do, madonna; but to read his right wits,
is to read thus: therefore perpend, my princess, and
give ear.

300 *Olivia* [*snatches the letter and gives it to Fabian*]. Read
it you, sirrah.

Fabian ['*reads*']. 'By the Lord, madam, you wrong me,
and the world shall know it: though you have put me
into darkness, and given your drunken cousin rule over
me, yet have I the benefit of my senses as well as your
ladyship. I have your own letter that induced me to the
semblance I put on; with the which I doubt not but to
do myself much right, or you much shame. Think of
me as you please. I leave my duty a little unthought of,
310 and speak out of my injury.

THE MADLY-USED MALVOLIO.'

Olivia. Did he write this?

Clown. Ay, madam.

Duke. This savours not much of distraction.

Olivia. See him delivered, Fabian, bring him hither...

[*Fabian goes within*

My lord, so please you, these things further thought on,
To think me as well a sister as a wife,
One day shall crown th'alliance on't, so please you,
Here at my house and at my proper cost.

Duke. Madam, I am most apt t'embrace your offer... 320
[*to Viola*] Your master quits you; and for your service
　　done him,
So much against the mettle of your sex,
So far beneath your soft and tender breeding,
And since you called me master for so long,
Here is my hand—you shall from this time be
Your master's mistress.
　　Olivia.　　　　　A sister! you are she.

FABIAN returns with MALVOLIO

Duke. Is this the madman?
　　Olivia.　　　　　Ay, my lord, this same:
How now, Malvolio?
　　Malvolio.　　　Madam, you have done me wrong,
Notorious wrong.
　　Olivia.　　　Have I, Malvolio? no!
　　Malvolio. Lady, you have. Pray you, peruse
　　　　that letter.... [*he takes a letter from his bosom* 330
You must not now deny it is your hand,
Write from it, if you can, in hand or phrase,
Or say 'tis not your seal, not your invention:
You can say none of this. Well, grant it then,
And tell me, in the modesty of honour,
Why you have given me such clear lights of favour,
Bade me come smiling and cross-gartered to you,
To put on yellow stockings and to frown
Upon Sir Toby and the lighter people:
And, acting this in an obedient hope,　　　　　340
Why have you suffered me to be imprisoned,
Kept in a dark house, visited by the priest,
And made the most notorious geck and gull
That e'er invention played on? tell me why.
　　Olivia. Alas, Malvolio, this is not my writing,
Though, I confess, much like the character:

But, out of question, 'tis Maria's hand.
And now I do bethink me, it was she
First told me thou wast mad; then cam'st in smiling,
350 And in such forms which here were presupposed
Upon thee in the letter...Prithee, be content—
This practice hath most shrewdly passed upon thee;
But, when we know the grounds and authors of it,
Thou shalt be both the plaintiff and the judge
Of thine own cause.

   Fabian.   Good madam, hear me speak;
And let no quarrel nor no brawl to come
Taint the condition of this present hour,
Which I have wond'red at. In hope it shall not,
Most freely I confess, myself and Toby
360 Set this device against Malvolio here,
Upon some stubborn and uncourteous parts
We had conceived in him: Maria writ
The letter at Sir Toby's great importance,
In recompense whereof he hath married her...
How with a sportful malice it was followed,
May rather pluck on laughter than revenge,
If that the injuries be justly weighed
That have on both sides passed.

   Olivia. Alas, poor fool! how have they baffled thee!
370   *Clown.* Why, 'Some are born great, some achieve
greatness, and some have greatness thrown upon them.'
I was one, sir, in this interlude, one Sir Topas, sir—but
that's all one...'By the Lord, fool, I am not mad!' But
do you remember? 'Madam, why laugh you at such a
barren rascal? an you smile not, he's gagged'...And thus
the whirligig of time brings in his revenges.

   Malvolio. I'll be revenged on the whole pack of you.

                   [he turns upon his heel and goes

   Olivia. He hath been most notoriously abused.

Duke. Pursue him, and entreat him to a peace:
He hath not told us of the captain yet.   380
When that is known, and golden time convents,
A solemn combination shall be made
Of our dear souls...Meantime, sweet sister,
We will not part from hence. Cesario, come!
For so you shall be, while you are a man;
But, when in other habits you are seen,
Orsino's mistress and his fancy's queen.

> [*all save the Clown go within*

Clown [*sings*].

    When that I was and a little tiny boy,
       With hey, ho, the wind and the rain:
    A foolish thing was but a toy,   390
       For the rain it raineth every day.

    But when I came to man's estate,
       With hey, ho, the wind and the rain:
    'Gainst knaves and thieves men shut their gate,
       For the rain it raineth every day.

    But when I came alas to wive,
       With hey, ho, the wind and the rain:
    By swaggering could I never thrive,
       For the rain it raineth every day.

    But when I came unto my beds,   400
       With hey, ho, the wind and the rain:
    With toss-pots still had drunken heads,
       For the rain it raineth every day.

    A great while ago the world begun,
       With hey, ho, the wind and the rain:
    But that's all one, our play is done,
       And we'll strive to please you every day.

> [*he goes*

WORDSWORTH CLASSICS

Other titles in this series

DISTRIBUTION

AUSTRALIA
Wordsworth Editions Ltd
c/o Axiom Distributors Pty Ltd
108-110 Rundle Street
Kent town
South Austrailia 5067

CANADA
Editions Phidal Inc
5518 Ferrier
Mont-Royal QC
Canada

DENMARK
Bog-fan/Bog Og Ide

FRANCE
Bookking International
16 Rue Des Grands Augustins
75006 Paris
France

GERMANY
Swan Buch-Vertrieb GmbH
Goldscheuerstrabe 16
D-7640 Kehl Am Rein
Germany

GREAT BRITAIN
Wordsworth Editions Ltd
8B East Street
Ware
Herts SG12 9HJ

HOLLAND & BELGIUM
Uitgeverlj En Boekhandel
Van Gennep BV
Spuistraat 283
1012 VR Amsterdam
Holland

IRELAND
Wordsworth Editions Ltd
c/o Roberts Books
Unit 12
Benson Street
Enterprise Centre
Hanover Quay
Dublin 2

NORWAY
Norsk Bokimport AS
Bertrand Narvesensvei 2
Postboks 6219
Etterstad
0602 Oslo
Norway

SOUTH AFRICA
Trade Winds Press (Pty) Ltd
P O Box 20194
Durban North 4016
South Africa